Deer Stands and Devotions: A Hunter's Walk with God

Joshua Rhoades

Published by Joshua Paul Rhoades, 2024.

While every precaution has been taken in the preparation of this book, the publisher assumes no responsibility for errors or omissions, or for damages resulting from the use of the information contained herein.

DEER STANDS AND DEVOTIONS: A HUNTER'S WALK WITH GOD

First edition. August 31, 2024.

ISBN: 979-8227713049

Written by Joshua Rhoades.

Also by Joshua Rhoades

Courage Under Fire: David's Stand On The Battlefield
Jonah's Journey: Voices Of Redemption And Lessons In Obedience
The Furnace Of Faith: 12 Principles From The Heat Of Faith
Whispers of Hope: Inspiring Stories of Men's Prayers In Scripture
Frontier Legends: The Oregon Dream
Elijah: A Beacon Of Boldness
HOOK, LINE & SAVIOUR - Faith Reflections from Fishing
Driven By Faith: Motor Racing Inspired Christian Life
30 Day Devotional - Bold and Strong- Coffee Devotions for a
Courageous Christian Walk
Authentic Christianity: The Heart of Old Time Religion
Consider The Ant - God's Tiny Preachers
Flee Fornication: The Plea For Purity
Renewed Hope- How to Find Encouragement in God
Sounding The Call - The Voice of Conviction
The Altar - Where Heaven Meets Earth
The Bible's Battlefields- Timeless Lessons from Ancient Wars
The Sacred Art of Silence - How Silence Speaks in Scripture
Under Fire- The Sanctity of the Traditional Biblical Home
Who Is on the Lord's Side? A Call to Righteousness
What Is Truth? - From Skepticism to Submission
First and Goal- Faith and Football Fundamentals
From Dugout to Devotion- Spiritual Lessons from Baseball
Par for the Course- Faith and Fairways
The Believer's Pace- Tools for Running Life's Marathon

The Immutable Fortress- Security in God's Unchanging Nature
Biblical Bravery
Deer Stands and Devotions: A Hunter's Walk with God
Jesus Knows- Our Hearts, Our Responsibility
Restoration - Setting The Bone
The Freedom of Forgiveness
The Jezebel Effect - Ancient Manipulations Modern Lessons
The Shout That Stopped The Saviour

Introduction

Conclusion

Introduction

"Deer Stands and Devotions: A Hunter's Walk with God" is more than just a book about hunting; it's a journey into the heart of creation and an exploration of the profound spiritual lessons that can be found in the quiet, reflective moments spent in nature. For many hunters, the time spent in a deer stand isn't just about the pursuit of game; it's a time to connect with God, to listen to His voice, and to reflect on His creation. This book is for those who see hunting not only as a sport but as an opportunity to deepen their relationship with the Creator.

In the stillness of a pre-dawn forest, as the world begins to wake up, there is a sense of awe that can only be felt in the presence of God's creation. The quiet rustle of leaves, the distant call of a bird, and the sight of a deer moving gracefully through the woods all serve as reminders of the intricate beauty of God's handiwork. These moments provide a unique backdrop for prayer, reflection, and meditation.

Hunting, in its purest form, requires patience, discipline, and a deep respect for nature. These qualities are also fundamental to a strong spiritual life. Just as a hunter must be patient, waiting for the right moment, a Christian must learn to wait on God's timing. The discipline required to prepare for a hunt mirrors the discipline needed in spiritual practices like prayer, fasting, and reading Scripture. And the respect a hunter has for the animal and the land reflects the reverence we should have for God and His creation. Through the experiences shared in this book, you will see how these parallels can enrich your walk with God.

"Deer Stands and Devotions" is not just for seasoned hunters, but for anyone who loves the outdoors and seeks to experience God in the midst of His creation. Whether you're a hunter looking to connect your passion for the sport with your faith, or someone seeking inspiration from the natural world, this book offers a perspective that is both refreshing and deeply spiritual.

As you read "Deer Stands and Devotions," you will be encouraged to see your time in the deer stand as more than just a pursuit of game, but as an opportunity for spiritual growth. You'll discover how the quiet moments in nature can become moments of profound connection with God, where every rustle of leaves and every breath of wind speaks of His presence. Whether you're in the woods or in the comfort of your home, this book will inspire you to walk with God in every season of life, drawing closer to Him as you experience the beauty and wonder of His creation.

Chapter 1 Discipline

Discipline is a fundamental aspect in both hunting and the Christian life, requiring a commitment to stay quiet, patient, and focused. For a hunter, discipline means being able to remain silent and still for extended periods, often in challenging weather conditions, while waiting for the perfect moment to take a shot. This requires immense self-control and patience, as any sudden movement or noise can scare away the game. Hunters must also be disciplined in their preparation, ensuring their gear is ready, and they are familiar with the terrain and behavior of their prey. This preparation involves learning about the habits and patterns of the animals they hunt, which can take years of study and experience. Additionally, hunters must adhere to laws and ethical guidelines to ensure the sustainability of wildlife populations and the safety of themselves and others. This level of discipline helps hunters to be successful and responsible, fostering a deep respect for nature and the environment.

In the Christian life, discipline is equally crucial, as it involves practicing spiritual disciplines that draw believers closer to God. These disciplines include regular prayer, Bible study, fasting, and attending church services. Just as a hunter prepares for the hunt, Christians prepare their hearts and minds through these practices, building a strong foundation of faith and knowledge. Prayer is a vital spiritual discipline, offering a way to communicate with God, seek guidance, and find peace. Regular Bible study helps Christians understand God's word and apply its teachings to their lives. Fasting is a discipline that helps believers focus on their spiritual growth by setting aside physical needs to concentrate on prayer and reflection. Attending church services provides a sense of community and accountability, encouraging believers to support one another in their faith journeys. These disciplines require commitment and perseverance, as they often involve setting aside time and effort in a busy world. The concept of discipline in both hunting and the Christian life is beautifully encapsulated in 1 Timothy 4:7, which says, "But refuse profane and old wives' fables, and exercise thyself rather unto godliness." This verse emphasizes the importance of focusing on what truly matters and exercising oneself in godliness, much like a hunter exercises patience and skill. In both realms, discipline is not just about following a set of rules but about cultivating habits and attitudes that lead to growth and success. For hunters, this means becoming more skilled and respectful of nature, while for Christians, it means growing closer to God and becoming more like Christ.

Discipline in hunting also involves physical fitness and mental toughness. Hunters often trek long distances through rough terrain, carry heavy gear, and endure extreme weather conditions. Maintaining physical fitness is essential to handle these challenges effectively. Mental toughness is equally important, as hunting can be a solitary and demanding activity that tests a person's patience and resilience. Hunters must remain focused and calm, even when faced with frustration or failure. This mental fortitude allows them to make clear and ethical decisions, ensuring a safe and successful hunt.

Similarly, in the Christian life, discipline encompasses physical and mental aspects. Maintaining one's physical health can be seen as a form of stewardship, taking care of the body that God has given. Mental discipline involves controlling one's thoughts, resisting temptation, and focusing on positive and godly influences. Christians are called to renew their minds and not conform to the patterns of this world, as stated in Romans 12:2: "And be not conformed to this world: but be ye transformed by the renewing of your mind, that ye may prove what is that good, and acceptable, and perfect, will of God." This mental renewal is achieved through continuous engagement with Scripture, prayer, and fellowship with other believers.

Furthermore, discipline in both hunting and the Christian life involves learning from experience and being open to growth. Hunters often learn from their successes and failures, continually refining their skills and strategies. This process of learning and adaptation is crucial for becoming a proficient hunter. Similarly, Christians grow through their experiences, learning from their mistakes, and seeking to improve their walk with God. This growth is facilitated by the Holy Spirit, who guides and teaches believers, helping them to become more Christ-like in their actions and attitudes.

Discipline also plays a role in how hunters and Christians handle challenges and adversity. For hunters, facing difficult conditions or unsuccessful hunts requires perseverance and a positive attitude. They must be able to push through disappointment and remain committed to their goals. This resilience is developed through practice and experience, teaching hunters to stay focused and determined. In the Christian life, believers face various trials and challenges that test their faith. James 1:2-4 encourages Christians to "count it all joy when ye fall into divers temptations; knowing this, that the trying of your faith worketh patience. But let patience have her perfect work, that ye may be perfect and entire, wanting nothing." This passage highlights the importance of perseverance and patience in the face of adversity, leading to spiritual maturity and completeness.

Another aspect of discipline in both hunting and the Christian life is the need for humility and teachability. Successful hunters are those who recognize that there is always more to learn and who are willing to seek advice and guidance from more experienced hunters. This humility allows them to grow and improve continually. Similarly, Christians are called to be humble and teachable, recognizing their dependence on God and the need for continual growth in their faith. Proverbs 3:5-6 advises believers to "Trust in the LORD with all thine heart; and lean not unto thine own understanding. In all thy ways acknowledge him, and he shall direct thy paths." This humility and trust in God are essential for spiritual growth and guidance.

Discipline in hunting also involves ethical considerations and a respect for wildlife. Ethical hunters follow regulations, respect hunting seasons, and aim to make clean, humane kills to minimize the suffering of animals. This ethical approach ensures the sustainability of wildlife populations and the preservation of natural habitats. It also reflects a broader respect for God's creation, recognizing the value and beauty of the natural world. Similarly, Christians are called to live ethically, following God's commandments and showing respect and love for others. This ethical living is a reflection of their faith and their commitment to following Jesus' example. Micah 6:8 sums up this call to ethical living: "He hath shewed thee, O man, what is good; and what doth the LORD require of thee, but to do justly, and to love mercy, and to walk humbly with thy God?"

In both hunting and the Christian life, discipline is a continuous journey, requiring dedication, perseverance, and a willingness to grow. For hunters, this journey involves mastering skills, respecting nature, and learning from experience. For Christians, it involves practicing spiritual disciplines, growing in faith, and living ethically according to God's word. Discipline is not about perfection but about commitment and progress, continually striving to improve and grow closer to the ultimate goal.

In conclusion, discipline is a cornerstone in both hunting and the Christian life, embodying patience, perseverance, humility, and ethical living. For hunters, discipline means staying quiet, being patient, and preparing meticulously for the hunt. It involves physical and mental toughness, learning from experience, and respecting ethical guidelines. For Christians, discipline means practicing spiritual disciplines like prayer and Bible study, maintaining physical and mental health, and growing in faith through trials and challenges. It also involves humility, teachability, and ethical living according to God's word. 1 Timothy 4:7 encapsulates this call to discipline: "But refuse profane and old wives' fables, and exercise thyself rather unto godliness." By embracing discipline in their respective pursuits, both hunters and Christians can achieve their goals, grow in their skills and faith, and live lives that honor God. Discipline is a journey marked by continuous effort, learning, and a commitment to excellence, leading to success and fulfillment in both hunting and the Christian life.

Chapter 2 Determination

Determination is an essential quality in both hunting and the Christian life, requiring persistence, patience, and unwavering focus. For hunters, determination means pursuing their game with relentless effort, even in the face of challenges and setbacks. Hunting is not always a straightforward or easy task; it often involves long hours of waiting, traversing difficult terrain, and dealing with adverse weather conditions. A determined hunter must stay focused and committed, not allowing fatigue or frustration to deter them from their goal. This level of commitment involves physical endurance, mental toughness, and a deep understanding of their environment and prey. Hunters often have to track animals over long distances, read subtle signs in nature, and make strategic decisions about when and how to approach their target. This determination drives them to keep going, even when success is not guaranteed and the process is arduous.

Similarly, in the Christian life, determination is crucial for running the race of faith with perseverance. Christians are called to live out their faith daily, striving to grow closer to God and to embody the teachings of Jesus. This spiritual journey is often likened to a race that requires endurance and steadfastness. Hebrews 12:1 captures this idea perfectly: "Let us run with patience the race that is set before us." This verse encourages believers to persevere in their faith, despite the obstacles and challenges they may encounter. The Christian life involves regular prayer, studying the Bible, and living according to God's commandments. These practices require determination, especially in a world that can be full of distractions and temptations.

For both hunters and Christians, determination involves setting clear goals and working diligently towards them. In hunting, this might mean planning the hunt, setting up the perfect spot, and waiting patiently for the right moment. For Christians, it means setting spiritual goals, such as deepening their prayer life, studying the

Scriptures more thoroughly, or committing to acts of service and kindness. Achieving these goals requires a focused and determined mindset.

Determination also involves overcoming setbacks. Hunters often face unsuccessful hunts, where despite their best efforts, they come back empty-handed. Instead of giving up, determined hunters learn from their experiences, refine their techniques, and try again. This resilience is crucial for long-term success. Similarly, Christians face spiritual setbacks, such as moments of doubt, temptation, or failure to live up to their own expectations. A determined Christian does not let these setbacks derail their faith; instead, they seek forgiveness, learn from their mistakes, and continue to strive towards their spiritual goals.

In both realms, determination is fueled by a sense of purpose. Hunters are often driven by the thrill of the hunt, the connection with nature, and the satisfaction of providing for their families. This sense of purpose keeps them motivated, even when the hunt is challenging. For Christians, the sense of purpose comes from their faith in God and their desire to live according to His will. They are motivated by the hope of eternal life, the desire to spread God's love, and the fulfillment that comes from living a life aligned with their beliefs.

Determination in hunting also involves preparation and strategy. Successful hunters meticulously prepare for their hunts, ensuring they have the right equipment, knowledge of the area, and understanding of their prey's behavior. This preparation is a testament to their determination to succeed. Similarly, Christians prepare for their spiritual journey through regular study of the Bible, prayer, and participation in church activities. This spiritual preparation strengthens their faith and equips them to face life's challenges with determination. Both hunters and Christians must also be patient. In hunting, patience is essential, as rushing can lead to mistakes and missed opportunities. A determined hunter knows that waiting for the right moment is crucial for a successful hunt. Similarly, Christians are called to be patient, trusting in God's timing and plan. They understand that spiritual growth and the fulfillment of God's promises often require waiting and perseverance. James 1:4 states, "But let patience have her perfect work, that ye may be perfect and entire, wanting nothing." This verse highlights the importance of patience in achieving spiritual maturity.

Another aspect of determination is adaptability. Hunters must adapt to changing conditions, such as weather, terrain, and the behavior of their prey. This adaptability is a key component of their determination to succeed. Similarly, Christians must adapt to life's changes and challenges while staying true to their faith. This requires a flexible yet steadfast approach, always seeking God's guidance in navigating life's uncertainties. Determination in hunting also includes teamwork. While hunting is often a solitary activity, it can also involve teamwork, where hunters work together, share knowledge, and support each other. This collective determination can lead to greater success. In the Christian life, fellowship and community are vital. Christians support each other through prayer, encouragement, and shared experiences. This sense of community strengthens their determination to live out their faith, knowing they are not alone in their journey.

Resilience is another critical component of determination. Hunters must be resilient in the face of physical and mental fatigue, learning to push through challenges and stay focused on their goal. This resilience is built through experience and a strong commitment to their passion for hunting. Similarly, Christians must be resilient in their faith, enduring trials and tribulations with hope and trust in God. Romans 5:3-4 says, "And not only so, but we glory in tribulations also: knowing that tribulation worketh patience; And patience, experience; and experience, hope." This passage emphasizes how trials can strengthen a believer's faith and build resilience.

Discipline is closely tied to determination. Hunters practice discipline in their approach, from maintaining their equipment to following hunting regulations and ethical guidelines. This discipline reflects their determination to hunt responsibly and successfully. In the Christian life, discipline is practiced through regular spiritual habits, such as prayer, fasting, and studying the Bible. These disciplines help Christians stay focused on their spiritual goals and maintain their determination to grow in their faith.

Both hunters and Christians must also navigate external influences and distractions. For hunters, this might include distractions from their surroundings or competing priorities. A determined hunter learns to stay focused and minimize distractions to achieve their goal. Similarly, Christians face numerous distractions in their daily lives, from societal pressures to personal challenges. Maintaining a determined focus on their faith requires setting boundaries and prioritizing their spiritual practices.

Determination also involves sacrifice. Hunters often sacrifice time, comfort, and convenience for the sake of the hunt. This sacrifice is a testament to their commitment and determination. In the Christian life, believers are called to make sacrifices, whether it be giving up certain habits, dedicating time to service, or making financial contributions to support their church and community. These sacrifices reflect their determination to live a life that honors God.

A determined hunter remains optimistic, even when faced with difficulties. This positive mindset helps them stay motivated and focused, believing that success is possible with perseverance. Similarly, Christians are encouraged to maintain a hopeful and positive attitude, trusting in God's promises and His plan for their lives. Romans 12:12 encourages believers to be "rejoicing in hope; patient in tribulation; continuing instant in prayer." This verse highlights the importance of maintaining hope and determination through constant communication with God.

Both hunters and Christians celebrate their successes and learn from their failures. For hunters, a successful hunt is a moment of celebration, while failures are opportunities for learning and improvement. This cycle of reflection and growth is driven by their determination to excel. Similarly, Christians celebrate their spiritual victories, such as overcoming temptations or reaching spiritual milestones, and learn from their mistakes. This reflective practice helps them grow in their faith and determination.

Lastly, determination in both hunting and the Christian life involves a deep sense of commitment and dedication. Hunters are deeply committed to their craft, continually seeking to improve and achieve their goals. This commitment is evident in their persistent efforts and unwavering focus. Similarly, Christians are called to be deeply committed to their faith, dedicating their lives to following God's will and serving others. This commitment is reflected in their consistent spiritual practices and their determination to live out their faith every day.

In conclusion, determination is a vital quality that drives success and growth in both hunting and the Christian life. For hunters, determination means pursuing their game with relentless effort, overcoming challenges, and continually seeking to improve. It involves patience, adaptability, resilience, discipline, and a positive mindset. For Christians, determination means running the race of faith with perseverance, setting spiritual goals, overcoming setbacks, and staying committed to their faith. It involves regular spiritual practices, trust in God's timing, adaptability to life's changes, resilience in the face of trials, and a deep sense of commitment and dedication. Hebrews 12:1 encapsulates this call to determination: "Let us run with patience the race that is set before us." By embracing determination in their respective pursuits, both hunters and Christians can achieve their goals, grow in their skills and faith, and live lives that honor God. Determination is a journey marked by continuous effort, learning, and a commitment to excellence, leading to success and fulfillment in both hunting and the Christian life.

Chapter 3 Dedication

Dedication is a key quality in both hunting and the Christian life, requiring a deep commitment, effort, and focus. For hunters, dedication means being committed to the entire process of hunting, which ensures better success. This dedication involves early mornings, long hours in often uncomfortable conditions, and meticulous preparation. Hunters spend considerable time studying animal behavior, learning the terrain, and honing their skills with their equipment. This preparation includes maintaining their gear, practicing their shooting accuracy, and understanding the regulations and ethical guidelines of hunting. A dedicated hunter also respects the environment and the wildlife, ensuring that they hunt responsibly and sustainably. This level of dedication often leads to greater success in hunting, as it involves a comprehensive approach to every aspect of the hunt. It's not just about the moment of the kill but about the entire journey, from preparation to execution to reflection.

Similarly, in the Christian life, dedication means being committed to serving God with all one's heart. Christians show their dedication through regular prayer, reading and studying the Bible, attending church, and living out their faith in daily life. Colossians 3:23 captures this dedication perfectly: "And whatsoever ye do, do it heartily, as to the Lord, and not unto men." This verse encourages believers to put their whole heart into whatever they do, working as if they are serving the Lord directly. This means that Christians are called to integrate their faith into every aspect of their lives, whether it's their work, relationships, or personal habits. Dedication to God involves a sincere commitment to grow spiritually, to love and serve others, and to strive to live according to God's will.

For both hunters and Christians, dedication involves a deep sense of purpose. Hunters are driven by a passion for the outdoors, the thrill of the hunt, and the satisfaction of providing for themselves or their families. This passion fuels their dedication, helping them to persevere through the challenges and difficulties that come with hunting. Similarly, Christians are driven by a desire to grow closer to God, to live out the teachings of Jesus, and to share God's love with others. This sense of purpose gives them the motivation and strength to remain dedicated to their faith, even in the face of trials and temptations.

Dedication in hunting also involves continuous learning and improvement. Hunters constantly seek to improve their skills and knowledge, learning from each hunting experience and adapting their strategies accordingly. They may spend time reading about hunting techniques, talking to more experienced hunters, and reflecting on their past hunts to identify areas for improvement. This dedication to continuous improvement helps them to become more skilled and successful hunters. Similarly, Christians are called to continually grow in their faith and understanding of God's word. This involves studying the Bible, participating in Bible studies and church activities, and seeking guidance from more mature Christians. By dedicating themselves to this continuous spiritual growth, Christians can deepen their relationship with God and become more effective in their witness and service to others.

Another aspect of dedication in both hunting and the Christian life is perseverance. Hunting often involves long periods of waiting and watching, sometimes in challenging conditions. A dedicated hunter perseveres through these difficulties, remaining focused and patient until the right opportunity arises. This perseverance is key to successful hunting, as it allows hunters to remain ready and alert, even when the wait is long. Similarly, Christians are called to persevere in their faith, even when faced with trials and hardships. James 1:12 says, "Blessed is the man that endureth temptation: for when he is tried, he shall receive the crown of life, which the Lord hath promised to them that love him." This verse encourages believers to remain steadfast and dedicated to God, knowing that their perseverance will be rewarded.

Dedication also involves sacrifice. Hunters often sacrifice their comfort, time, and sometimes even their safety to pursue their passion for hunting. This sacrifice is a testament to their dedication and commitment to the hunt. Similarly, Christians are called to make sacrifices in their dedication to God. This might involve giving up certain habits or lifestyle choices, dedicating time to serve others, or making financial contributions to support their church and community. Romans 12:1 says, "I beseech you therefore, brethren, by the mercies of God, that ye present your bodies a living sacrifice, holy, acceptable unto God, which is your reasonable service." This verse highlights the idea that true dedication to God involves a willingness to offer one's entire life as a sacrifice, living in a way that honors and serves God.

In both hunting and the Christian life, dedication is also reflected in how one handles challenges and setbacks. For hunters, this might mean dealing with unsuccessful hunts, harsh weather, or physical exhaustion. A dedicated hunter does not give up but learns from these experiences and continues to pursue their goals with determination and resilience. Similarly, Christians face spiritual challenges, such as doubts, temptations, and hardships. A dedicated Christian remains steadfast in their faith, seeking God's guidance and strength to overcome these challenges. Philippians 4:13 says, "I can do all things through Christ which strengtheneth me." This verse reminds believers that their dedication to God is supported by His strength, enabling them to persevere through any difficulty.

Both hunters and Christians also demonstrate their dedication through their commitment to ethical behavior and integrity. For hunters, this means following hunting regulations, respecting wildlife, and practicing fair chase principles. Ethical hunting ensures the sustainability of wildlife populations and reflects a deep respect for nature. This integrity is a key aspect of their dedication to the sport. Similarly, Christians are called to live with integrity, following God's commandments and living in a way that reflects their faith. This involves being honest, kind, and just in all their interactions, and striving to live a life that honors God. Micah 6:8 says, "He hath shewed thee, O man, what is good; and what doth the LORD require of thee, but to do justly, and to love mercy, and to walk humbly with thy God?" This verse encapsulates the ethical and moral standards that Christians are called to uphold in their dedication to God.

Dedication in both hunting and the Christian life also involves a sense of community and support. Hunters often share their experiences, knowledge, and tips with each other, creating a community of mutual support and learning. This sense of camaraderie enhances their dedication and enjoyment of the sport. Similarly, Christians are part of a faith community that supports and encourages one another. Hebrews 10:24-25 says, "And let us consider one another to provoke unto love and to good works: Not forsaking the assembling of ourselves together, as the manner of some is; but exhorting one another: and so much the more, as ye see the day approaching." This verse highlights the importance of fellowship and mutual encouragement in maintaining dedication to the Christian faith.

Another important aspect of dedication is the willingness to take on responsibility. In hunting, this might mean ensuring that all equipment is well-maintained, that safety measures are followed, and that the hunter is knowledgeable about the area and the prey. This responsibility reflects a deep dedication to the hunt and to the principles of ethical hunting. Similarly, Christians are called to take on responsibilities within their faith communities and in their personal lives. This might involve teaching, mentoring, serving in church roles, or simply being a positive example to others. 1 Peter 4:10 says, "As every man hath received the gift, even so minister the same one to another, as good stewards of the manifold grace of God." This verse encourages believers to use their gifts and talents in service to others, demonstrating their dedication to God through their actions.

In both hunting and the Christian life, dedication is often accompanied by a deep sense of satisfaction and fulfillment. For hunters, the success of a well-planned and executed hunt brings a sense of accomplishment and joy. This satisfaction is not just about the hunt itself but about the entire process and the dedication it represents. Similarly, Christians find deep fulfillment in their relationship with God and in living out their faith. This fulfillment comes from knowing that they are living according to God's will and making a positive impact in the world. Psalm 37:4 says, "Delight thyself also in the LORD; and he shall give thee the desires of thine heart." This verse highlights the joy and satisfaction that come from a dedicated relationship with God.

In conclusion, dedication is a cornerstone of success and fulfillment in both hunting and the Christian life. For hunters, dedication means committing fully to the hunt, from preparation to execution, and continuously seeking to improve and respect the environment. It involves perseverance, sacrifice, ethical behavior, and a sense of community. For Christians, dedication means serving God with all one's heart, integrating faith into every aspect of life, and striving for continuous spiritual growth. It involves regular prayer, Bible study, ethical living, and a commitment to community and service. Colossians 3:23 encapsulates this call to dedication: "And whatsoever ye do, do it heartily, as to the Lord, and not unto men." By embracing dedication in their respective pursuits, both hunters and Christians can achieve their goals, grow in their skills and faith, and live lives that honor God. Dedication is a journey marked by continuous effort, learning, and a commitment to excellence, leading to success and fulfillment in both hunting and the Christian life.

Chapter 4 Diligence

Diligence is an essential trait in both hunting and the Christian life, involving persistent effort, careful observation, and unwavering commitment. For hunters, diligence means being meticulous in tracking and observing their prey. This requires a deep understanding of animal behavior, habitats, and movement patterns. Hunters must pay close attention to tracks, droppings, sounds, and other signs that indicate the presence of their target. This process can be time-consuming and requires patience and perseverance. A diligent hunter will spend hours, days, or even weeks studying the terrain and the habits of the animals they pursue, ensuring that they are in the right place at the right time. They must also be meticulous in preparing their equipment, maintaining their weapons, and ensuring that their camouflage is effective. This level of diligence increases their chances of a successful hunt and reflects their commitment to the craft.

Similarly, in the Christian life, diligence is crucial for spiritual growth and maturity. Christians are called to be diligent in their pursuit of godliness, continuously seeking to grow in their faith and understanding of God's word. This involves regular prayer, Bible study, and participation in church activities. Just as a hunter carefully observes the signs of their prey, Christians must be attentive to the guidance of the Holy Spirit, the teachings of the Bible, and the counsel of wise mentors. 2 Peter 1:5-6 encourages believers to "give all diligence, add to your faith virtue; and to virtue knowledge; and to knowledge temperance; and to temperance patience; and to patience godliness." This passage highlights the importance of diligence in developing a well-rounded and mature faith. Each aspect of spiritual growth builds upon the other, and diligent effort is required to cultivate these qualities.

For both hunters and Christians, diligence involves a continuous commitment to learning and improvement. Hunters continually refine their skills, learning from each hunting experience and seeking out new knowledge and techniques. This might involve reading books, watching instructional videos, or seeking advice from more experienced hunters. Diligence in learning ensures that hunters remain adaptable and effective in various hunting scenarios. Similarly, Christians are called to be lifelong learners, continually deepening their understanding of the Bible and their relationship with God. This involves regular study of Scripture, participation in Bible studies and small groups, and seeking out opportunities for spiritual growth and development. By diligently pursuing knowledge and understanding, Christians can grow in their faith and become more effective in living out their beliefs.

Another important aspect of diligence is perseverance. Hunting often involves long periods of waiting and careful observation, and it can be easy to become discouraged or lose focus. A diligent hunter perseveres through these challenges, remaining patient and committed even when success seems elusive. This perseverance is essential for achieving their goals and reflects their dedication to the hunt. Similarly, Christians are called to persevere in their faith, even in the face of trials and difficulties. James 1:12 says, "Blessed is the man that endureth temptation: for when he is tried, he shall receive the crown of life, which the Lord hath promised to them that love him." This verse encourages believers to remain steadfast in their faith, trusting that their diligent efforts will be rewarded.

Diligence also involves attention to detail. Hunters must be meticulous in their observations and preparations, ensuring that they do not overlook any signs or details that could be crucial to their success. This attention to detail helps them to make informed decisions and increases their chances of a successful hunt. Similarly, Christians are called to be diligent in their spiritual practices, paying close attention to their thoughts, actions, and attitudes. This involves regular self-examination and a commitment to living according to God's word. Psalm 119:105 says, "Thy word is a lamp unto my feet, and a light unto my path." This verse highlights the importance of diligently studying and applying Scripture to guide one's life.

In both hunting and the Christian life, diligence is also reflected in how one handles setbacks and challenges. For hunters, this might mean dealing with missed opportunities, harsh weather, or difficult terrain. A diligent hunter does not give up but learns from these experiences and continues to pursue their goals with determination. Similarly, Christians face spiritual challenges, such as doubts, temptations, and hardships. A diligent Christian remains steadfast in their faith, seeking God's guidance and strength to overcome these challenges. Philippians 4:13 says, "I can do all things through Christ which strengtheneth me." This verse reminds believers that their diligence in pursuing godliness is supported by God's strength, enabling them to persevere through any difficulty.

Diligence in both hunting and the Christian life also involves a commitment to ethical behavior and integrity. For hunters, this means following hunting regulations, respecting wildlife, and practicing fair chase principles. Ethical hunting ensures the sustainability of wildlife populations and reflects a deep respect for nature. This integrity is a key aspect of their diligence in the sport. Similarly, Christians are called to live with integrity, following God's commandments and living in a way that reflects their faith. This involves being honest, kind, and just in all their interactions, and striving to live a life that honors God. Micah 6:8 says, "He hath shewed thee, O man, what is good; and what doth the LORD require of thee, but to do justly, and to love mercy, and to walk humbly with thy God?" This verse encapsulates the ethical and moral standards that Christians are called to uphold in their diligence.

Both hunters and Christians also demonstrate their diligence through their commitment to community and mutual support.

Hunters often share their experiences, knowledge, and tips with each other, creating a community of mutual support and learning. This sense of camaraderie enhances their diligence and enjoyment of the sport. Similarly, Christians are part of a faith community that supports and encourages one another. Hebrews 10:24-25 says, "And let us consider one another to provoke unto love and to good works: Not forsaking the assembling of ourselves together, as the manner of some is; but exhorting one another: and so much the more, as ye see the day approaching." This verse highlights the importance of fellowship and mutual encouragement in maintaining diligence in the Christian faith.

Diligence also involves a sense of responsibility. In hunting, this means ensuring that all equipment is well-maintained, that safety measures are followed, and that the hunter is knowledgeable about the area and the prey. This responsibility reflects a deep diligence to the hunt and to the principles of ethical hunting. Similarly, Christians are called to take on responsibilities within their faith communities and in their personal lives. This might involve teaching, mentoring, serving in church roles, or simply being a positive example to others. 1 Peter 4:10 says, "As every man hath received the gift, even so minister the same one to another, as good stewards of the manifold grace of God." This verse encourages believers to use their gifts and talents in service to others, demonstrating their diligence to God through their actions.

In both hunting and the Christian life, diligence is often accompanied by a deep sense of satisfaction and fulfillment. For hunters, the success of a well-planned and executed hunt brings a sense of accomplishment and joy. This satisfaction is not just about the hunt itself but about the entire process and the diligence it represents. Similarly, Christians find deep fulfillment in their relationship with God and in living out their faith. This fulfillment comes from knowing that they are living according to God's will and making a positive impact in the world. Psalm 37:4 says, "Delight thyself also in the LORD; and he shall give thee the desires of thine heart." This verse highlights the joy and satisfaction that come from a diligent relationship with God.

Diligence in hunting also involves continuous adaptation and flexibility. Hunters must be able to adapt to changing conditions, such as weather, terrain, and the behavior of their prey. This adaptability is a key component of their diligence, allowing them to remain effective in various hunting scenarios. Similarly, Christians must be adaptable in their spiritual journey, remaining open to the leading of the Holy Spirit and willing to adjust their plans according to God's will. Proverbs 16:9 says, "A man's heart deviseth his way: but the LORD directeth his steps." This verse highlights the importance of trusting in God's guidance and being diligent in following His direction.

In conclusion, diligence is a cornerstone of success and fulfillment in both hunting and the Christian life. For hunters, diligence means committing fully to the hunt, from preparation to execution, and continuously seeking to improve and respect the environment. It involves perseverance, attention to detail, ethical behavior, and a sense of community. For Christians, diligence means pursuing godliness with all one's heart, integrating faith into every aspect of life, and striving for continuous spiritual growth. It involves regular prayer, Bible study, ethical living, and a commitment to community and service. 2 Peter 1:5-6 encapsulates this call to diligence: "And beside this, giving all diligence, add to your faith virtue; and to virtue knowledge; and to knowledge temperance; and to temperance patience; and to patience godliness." By embracing diligence in their respective pursuits, both hunters and Christians can achieve their goals, grow in their skills and faith, ded live lives that honor God. Diligence is a journey marked by continuous effort, learning, and a commitment to excellence, leading to success and fulfillment in both hunting and the Christian life.

Chapter 5 Dependence

Dependence is a vital aspect of both hunting and the Christian life, encompassing reliance on resources, skills, and guidance beyond oneself. In hunting, hunters depend heavily on their gear and skills to be successful. This includes a deep reliance on their weapons, such as rifles, bows, and ammunition, ensuring these tools are well-maintained and functioning correctly. Hunters also depend on their knowledge and expertise, developed through years of practice and learning. This expertise includes understanding animal behavior, reading signs in nature, and making strategic decisions about when and where to hunt. Weather conditions, terrain, and the behavior of the prey all play a crucial role in the hunt, and hunters must be adaptable and resourceful, depending on their skills and gear to navigate these challenges. Furthermore, hunters often rely on the camaraderie and support of fellow hunters, sharing knowledge and experiences to enhance their skills and improve their chances of success. This sense of community and mutual dependence helps hunters to grow and develop, learning from each other and building a network of support and collaboration.

Similarly, in the Christian life, dependence is centered on trusting in God for strength, guidance, and provision. Christians are called to rely not on their own understanding but on God's wisdom and direction. Proverbs 3:5-6 perfectly captures this dependence: "Trust in the LORD with all thine heart; and lean not unto thine own understanding. In all thy ways acknowledge him, and he shall direct thy paths." This verse encourages believers to place their trust entirely in God, acknowledging His sovereignty and seeking His guidance in all aspects of life. Dependence on God involves a deep and abiding trust that He is in control, that His plans are perfect, and that He will provide for all needs. This trust is cultivated through regular prayer, reading the Bible, and being attentive to the leading of the Holy Spirit. Just as a hunter depends on their gear and skills, Christians depend on their relationship with God to navigate life's challenges and uncertainties.

In both hunting and the Christian life, dependence involves preparation and readiness. For hunters, this means ensuring their equipment is in top condition, practicing their skills regularly, and being prepared for any situation that may arise during the hunt. This preparation reflects a dependence on their gear and abilities to succeed. Similarly, Christians prepare for their spiritual journey through regular study of Scripture, prayer, and engagement with their faith community. This preparation helps them to remain strong and focused, depending on God's word and His promises to guide them through life's trials. Dependence on God also involves acknowledging human limitations and the need for divine intervention. Just as hunters recognize that they cannot control every aspect of the hunt and must adapt to changing conditions, Christians acknowledge their own limitations and rely on God's strength and wisdom to overcome challenges. This humility and recognition of one's own need for God's guidance is a key aspect of dependence in the Christian life.

Dependence also involves trust and faith. Hunters must trust in their skills and gear, believing that their preparation and knowledge will lead to success. This trust is built through experience and practice, as hunters learn to rely on their abilities and tools in various situations. Similarly, Christians are called to have faith in God, trusting that He will guide and support them through all circumstances. Hebrews 11:1 defines faith as "the substance of things hoped for, the evidence of things not seen." This faith is the foundation of dependence on God, allowing believers to trust in His plans even when they cannot see the outcome. Dependence on God involves a deep-seated belief that He is faithful and that His promises are true.

In both realms, dependence also encompasses a sense of community and mutual support. Hunters often rely on the support and knowledge of fellow hunters, learning from each other and working together to achieve their goals. This community of hunters provides a network of support, encouragement, and shared experiences that enhance their abilities and success. Similarly, Christians are part of a faith community that supports and encourages one another. This community provides a source of strength, wisdom, and accountability, helping believers to grow in their faith and dependence on God. Hebrews 10:24-25 highlights the importance of this community: "And let us consider one another to provoke unto love and to good works: Not forsaking the assembling of ourselves together, as the manner of some is; but exhorting one another: and so much the more, as ye see the day approaching." This verse emphasizes the role of community in fostering dependence on God and encouraging spiritual growth.

Another important aspect of dependence is adaptability. Hunters must be adaptable, relying on their skills and gear to navigate changing conditions and unexpected challenges. This adaptability is a key component of their dependence, allowing them to remain effective and successful in various hunting scenarios. Similarly, Christians must be adaptable in their spiritual journey, remaining open to the leading of the Holy Spirit and willing to adjust their plans according to God's will. Dependence on God involves trusting His guidance and being willing to follow His direction, even when it leads to unexpected or challenging situations. This adaptability reflects a deep trust in God's sovereignty and a willingness to submit to His plans.

Dependence also involves a deep sense of gratitude. Hunters often express gratitude for the success of a hunt, recognizing the factors beyond their control that contributed to their success. This gratitude reflects an acknowledgment of the support and resources that made the hunt possible. Similarly, Christians are called to express gratitude to God for His provision and guidance. This gratitude is a key aspect of dependence, as it acknowledges God's role in providing for all needs and guiding one's path. 1 Thessalonians 5:18 encourages believers to "give thanks in all circumstances; for this is the will of God in Christ

Jesus for you." This gratitude fosters a deeper dependence on God, recognizing His constant presence and provision.

In both hunting and the Christian life, dependence is also reflected in the way one handles challenges and setbacks. Hunters must rely on their skills and knowledge to overcome difficulties, learning from each experience and adapting their strategies. This resilience and adaptability are key components of their dependence, allowing them to persevere and succeed. Similarly, Christians are called to depend on God's strength and guidance in the face of trials and difficulties. This dependence involves trusting that God is in control and that He will provide the strength and wisdom needed to overcome challenges. Philippians 4:13 says, "I can do all things through Christ which strengtheneth me." This verse reminds believers that their dependence on God is supported by His strength, enabling them to persevere through any difficulty.

Dependence in both hunting and the Christian life also involves a commitment to ethical behavior and integrity. Hunters rely on their commitment to ethical hunting practices, ensuring that they respect wildlife and follow hunting regulations. This ethical behavior reflects their dependence on a set of principles that guide their actions and ensure the sustainability of wildlife populations. Similarly, Christians are called to live with integrity, following God's commandments and living in a way that reflects their faith. This involves being honest, kind, and just in all their interactions, and striving to live a life that honors God. Micah 6:8 encapsulates this ethical call: "He hath shewed thee, O man, what is good; and what doth the LORD require of thee, but to do justly, dear to love mercy, and to walk humbly with thy God?" This verse highlights the ethical and moral standards that Christians are called to uphold in their dependence on God.

Both hunters and Christians also demonstrate their dependence through their commitment to continuous learning and improvement. Hunters continually seek to improve their skills and knowledge, learning from each hunting experience and seeking out new techniques and strategies. This commitment to continuous learning reflects their dependence on a broad base of knowledge and expertise. Similarly, Christians are called to be lifelong learners, continually deepening their understanding of the Bible and their relationship with God. This involves regular study of Scripture, participation in Bible studies and small groups, and seeking out opportunities for spiritual growth and development. By diligently pursuing knowledge and understanding, Christians can grow in their faith and become more effective in living out their beliefs.

Dependence also involves recognizing and embracing one's limitations. Hunters understand that they cannot control every aspect of the hunt and must rely on their skills and gear to navigate the uncertainties. This recognition of limitations is a key aspect of their dependence, allowing them to remain focused and adaptable. Similarly, Christians acknowledge their own limitations and rely on God's strength and wisdom to overcome challenges. This humility and recognition of one's own need for God's guidance is a key aspect of dependence in the Christian life. Psalm 121:1-2 says, "I will lift up mine eyes unto the hills, from whence cometh my help. My help cometh from the LORD, which made heaven and earth." This verse highlights the importance of looking to God for help and guidance, acknowledging His role as the ultimate source of strength and support.

In conclusion, dependence is a cornerstone of success and fulfillment in both hunting and the Christian life. For hunters, dependence means relying on their gear, skills, and knowledge to navigate the challenges of the hunt. It involves preparation, adaptability, community support, and a commitment to ethical behavior. For Christians, dependence means trusting in God for strength, guidance, and provision. It involves regular prayer, Bible study, ethical living, and a commitment to community and continuous learning. Proverbs 3:5-6 encapsulates this call to dependence: "Trust in the LORD with all thine heart; and lean not unto thine own understanding. In all thy ways acknowledge him, and he shall direct thy paths." By embracing dependence in their respective pursuits, both hunters and Christians can achieve their goals, grow in their skills and faith, and live lives that honor God. Dependence is a journey marked by continuous effort, learning, and a commitment to humility and trust, leading to success and fulfillment in both hunting and the Christian life.

Chapter 6 Disguise

Disguise plays a crucial role in both hunting and the Christian life, with hunters using camouflage to blend into their environment and Christians called to live in the world without becoming part of it. For hunters, disguise involves wearing clothing and gear that matches the natural surroundings, helping them remain undetected by their prey. This camouflage can include patterned clothing, face paint, and even scent masking to avoid alerting animals to their presence. By blending into the environment, hunters can move closer to their targets without being noticed, increasing their chances of a successful hunt. This careful attention to disguise requires knowledge of the terrain and the behavior of the animals they are hunting, as different environments and species require different camouflage techniques. Hunters must remain still and quiet, fully integrating with the natural world around them to become almost invisible. This level of disguise is not just about the clothing but also about the hunter's ability to adapt their movements and behavior to avoid detection. The art of disguise in hunting is a testament to the hunter's skill, patience, and understanding of the natural world, highlighting the intricate relationship between humans and nature.

In the Christian life, disguise takes on a different but equally important meaning. Christians are called to be in the world but not of the world, a concept that involves living among others without conforming to worldly values and behaviors that contradict their faith. This idea is beautifully captured in John 17:15-16, where Jesus prays, "I pray not that thou shouldest take them out of the world, but that thou shouldest keep them from the evil. They are not of the world, even as I am not of the world." This verse underscores the Christian's role to engage with the world while maintaining their distinct identity and values rooted in their faith. Just as hunters use camouflage to blend in while remaining focused on their goal, Christians are called to live in a way that reflects their faith without being influenced by negative societal norms. This means upholding Christian values of love, honesty, humility, and integrity, even when these values are countercultural. It involves being a light in the darkness, showing others the love of Christ through actions and words while not adopting behaviors that go against biblical teachings.

For both hunters and Christians, disguise requires a balance between blending in and maintaining one's core identity. In hunting, the goal is to become part of the environment to achieve success, but the hunter's identity and purpose remain clear. Similarly, Christians live among others, participating in daily life, work, and community, but their faith guides their actions and decisions. This balance is crucial for maintaining integrity and effectiveness in their respective roles. For hunters, it means using their disguise to get closer to their prey while ensuring they hunt ethically and responsibly. For Christians, it means engaging with the world to make a positive impact without compromising their beliefs and values. This balance is achieved through a strong foundation of knowledge, practice, and continuous reflection, allowing both hunters and Christians to navigate their environments effectively.

In hunting, disguise also involves understanding the behavior and perception of animals. Different species have different visual capabilities and senses, requiring hunters to adapt their camouflage strategies accordingly. This knowledge allows hunters to choose the right patterns and colors, remain still, and move in ways that mimic natural movements in the environment. This careful adaptation shows the hunter's respect for the natural world and their commitment to ethical hunting practices. Similarly, Christians are called to understand the world around them and engage with it thoughtfully. This involves being aware of societal issues, cultural dynamics, and the needs of others, allowing Christians to respond with empathy, wisdom, and love. By understanding the world, Christians can better communicate their faith and serve their communities, making a meaningful impact without losing their identity.

Disguise in hunting also requires preparation and planning. Hunters spend time preparing their gear, studying the terrain, and understanding the habits of their prey. This preparation ensures that they can effectively blend into their environment and remain undetected. Similarly, Christians prepare themselves spiritually through prayer, Bible study, and fellowship with other believers. This spiritual preparation strengthens their faith and equips them to face the challenges of living in a world that often opposes their values. By grounding themselves in their faith, Christians can navigate their environment with confidence and resilience, staying true to their beliefs while engaging with the world.

Both hunters and Christians must also deal with the challenges and temptations that come with disguise. For hunters, the temptation might be to cut corners or use methods that are not ethical, such as baiting or spotlighting. A committed hunter adheres to ethical guidelines, ensuring that their disguise is used in a way that respects the animal and the environment. This ethical approach fosters a deeper respect for nature and promotes sustainable hunting practices. For Christians, the temptation might be to conform to societal pressures or compromise their values to fit in. A dedicated Christian remains steadfast in their faith, using their engagement with the world to reflect Christ's love and truth without succumbing to negative influences. This steadfastness is rooted in a deep trust in God and a commitment to living according to His word.

Disguise also involves a sense of humility and teachability. Hunters must be humble enough to learn from their experiences, adapt their strategies, and seek advice from more experienced hunters. This humility allows them to improve their skills and become more effective in their craft. Similarly, Christians are called to be humble, recognizing their dependence on God and being open to learning and growth. This humility involves listening to God's guidance, seeking wisdom from Scripture, and being receptive to the counsel of other believers. By maintaining a teachable spirit, Christians can grow in their faith and better navigate the challenges of living in the world.

In both hunting and the Christian life, disguise is not about deception but about strategic engagement. Hunters use camouflage to engage more effectively with their environment, ensuring a successful hunt while respecting the natural world. Christians engage with the world strategically, living out their faith in a way that influences others positively without compromising their values. This strategic engagement requires discernment, wisdom, and a clear sense of purpose. By understanding their role and staying true to their core identity, both hunters and Christians can navigate their environments effectively and make a meaningful impact.

Disguise in hunting also highlights the importance of patience and perseverance. Hunters must often wait for long periods, remaining still and quiet, to avoid detection and increase their chances of success. This patience is a testament to their dedication and commitment to the hunt. Similarly, Christians are called to be patient and persevere in their faith, even when faced with challenges and opposition. James 1:12 says, "Blessed is the man that endureth temptation: for when he is tried, he shall receive the crown of life, which the Lord hath promised to them that love him." This verse encourages believers to remain steadfast, trusting that their perseverance will be rewarded.

Both hunters and Christians also rely on a community for support and encouragement. Hunters often share their experiences and knowledge with each other, creating a network of support and collaboration. This sense of community enhances their skills and fosters a deeper appreciation for the art of hunting. Similarly, Christians are part of a faith community that supports and encourages one another. This community provides strength, wisdom, and accountability, helping believers to stay true to their faith and navigate the challenges of living in the world. Hebrews 10:24-25 highlights the importance of this community: "And let us consider one another to provoke unto love and to good works: Not forsaking the assembling of ourselves together, as the manner of some is; but exhorting one another: and so much the more, as ye see the day approaching."

In both hunting and the Christian life, disguise also involves a commitment to ethical behavior and integrity. Hunters adhere to ethical hunting practices, ensuring that they respect wildlife and follow regulations. This integrity reflects their commitment to ethical principles and fosters a deeper respect for nature. Similarly, Christians are called to live with integrity, following God's commandments and reflecting their faith in their actions. This involves being honest, kind, and just in all their interactions, striving to live a life that honors God. Micah 6:8 encapsulates this ethical call: "He hath shewed thee, O man, what is good; and what doth the LORD require of thee, but to do justly, and to love mercy, and to walk humbly with thy God?"

Both hunters and Christians demonstrate their commitment through continuous learning and improvement. Hunters continually seek to improve their skills and knowledge, learning from each experience and adapting their strategies. This commitment to continuous learning reflects their dedication to the craft. Similarly, Christians are called to be lifelong learners, continually deepening their understanding of the Bible and their relationship with God. This involves regular study of Scripture, participation in Bible studies and small groups, and seeking opportunities for spiritual growth and development. By diligently pursuing knowledge and understanding, Christians can grow in their faith and become more effective in living out their beliefs.

In conclusion, disguise plays a crucial role in both hunting and the Christian life, encompassing the use of camouflage and strategic engagement to achieve success and maintain integrity. For hunters, disguise involves blending into the environment through camouflage, remaining undetected by their prey, and adhering to ethical hunting practices. It requires patience, perseverance, and a deep understanding of the natural world. For Christians, disguise means living in the world without conforming to it, engaging with society in a way that reflects their faith and values. It involves maintaining integrity, relying on a supportive community, and continuously seeking to grow in their relationship with God. John 17:15-16 encapsulates this call to be in the world but not of it: "I pray not that thou shouldest take them out of the world, but that thou shouldest keep them from the evil. They are not of the world, even as I am not of the world." By embracing the principles of disguise in their respective pursuits, both hunters and Christians can achieve their goals, grow in their skills and faith, and live lives that honor God. Disguise is a journey marked by continuous effort, learning, and a commitment to ethical behavior and integrity, leading to success and fulfillment in both hunting and the Christian life.

Chapter 7 Direction

Direction is an essential element in both hunting and the Christian life, requiring a clear path, guidance, and the ability to navigate challenges effectively. For hunters, having a clear sense of direction is crucial to successfully navigating the wild. This involves understanding the terrain, using maps or GPS devices, and being able to read natural signs like the position of the sun, animal tracks, and changes in the landscape. Hunters must plan their routes carefully, knowing where they want to go and how to get there without getting lost. This sense of direction helps them locate their prey, find safe paths, and return home safely. It involves not only physical navigation but also strategic planning, such as determining the best spots to set up blinds or tree stands based on wind direction and animal behavior. Hunters also need to be able to adapt their direction based on changing conditions, such as weather or unexpected obstacles, demonstrating flexibility and problem-solving skills. A clear sense of direction is built on knowledge, experience, and the ability to stay focused on the goal, ensuring that the hunter can move through the wilderness with confidence and purpose.

Similarly, in the Christian life, seeking God's direction is essential for living a life that aligns with His will and purpose. Christians look to God for guidance in their decisions, actions, and overall path in life. This direction is found through prayer, reading the Bible, and listening to the Holy Spirit. Psalm 32:8 beautifully captures this divine guidance: "I will instruct thee and teach thee in the way which thou shalt go: I will guide thee with mine eye." This verse emphasizes that God is always willing to lead His followers, providing instruction and insight for the journey ahead. Just as hunters need to understand the terrain and plan their routes, Christians need to seek God's wisdom to navigate the complexities of life. This involves trusting in His plans, even when they are not fully understood, and being open to His leading. By following God's direction, Christians can make choices that honor Him and reflect His love and grace to others. This divine guidance helps them avoid spiritual pitfalls, overcome challenges, and stay on the path that leads to eternal life with God.

For both hunters and Christians, direction involves preparation and intentionality. Hunters prepare by studying maps, learning about the behavior of their prey, and ensuring they have the necessary equipment to navigate the wilderness. This preparation allows them to move with confidence, knowing that they are ready to face any obstacles that may arise. Similarly, Christians prepare by spending time in prayer, studying the Bible, and seeking the counsel of wise and godly mentors. This spiritual preparation equips them to follow God's direction, providing clarity and strength to face life's challenges. By grounding themselves in God's word and being attentive to His voice, Christians can navigate their journey with purpose and assurance.

Direction also involves the ability to adapt and respond to changing circumstances. Hunters must be able to adjust their course if they encounter unexpected barriers or if their prey changes its pattern. This flexibility is a key aspect of effective navigation, allowing hunters to stay on track even when conditions shift. Similarly, Christians must be open to adjusting their plans based on God's leading. Life is full of unexpected twists and turns, and a rigid approach can lead to frustration and missteps. By remaining flexible and trusting in God's sovereignty, Christians can adapt to new situations while staying aligned with God's direction. Proverbs 16:9 says, "A man's heart deviseth his way: but the LORD directeth his steps." This verse highlights the importance of being open to God's guidance, recognizing that His plans are higher and more perfect than our own.

In both hunting and the Christian life, direction also requires patience and perseverance. Hunters often need to travel long distances, sometimes through difficult terrain, requiring endurance and determination to reach their destination. They must be patient, knowing that the journey is part of the process and that each step brings them closer to their goal. Similarly, Christians are called to persevere in their faith, trusting in God's timing and remaining steadfast even when the path is difficult. Hebrews 12:1 encourages believers to "run with patience the race that is set before us." This perseverance is fueled by the assurance that God is guiding them and that He has a perfect plan for their lives.

Both hunters and Christians also rely on tools and resources to aid in their navigation. For hunters, this might include maps, compasses, GPS devices, and tracking tools that help them stay oriented and find their way. These tools are essential for ensuring they do not get lost and can reach their destination safely. Similarly, Christians have spiritual tools that help them stay on course. The Bible serves as a map, providing wisdom and guidance for life's journey. Prayer is a compass, aligning their hearts with God's will and keeping them focused on His direction. The Holy Spirit acts as a guide, providing insight and conviction to help believers make wise decisions. By utilizing these spiritual tools, Christians can navigate their lives with confidence and clarity, knowing that they are following the path God has set for them.

Community and mentorship also play a significant role in providing direction. Hunters often learn from more experienced hunters, gaining knowledge and skills that help them navigate the wilderness more effectively. This mentorship provides valuable insights and encouragement, helping novice hunters grow and succeed. Similarly, Christians benefit from being part of a faith community where they can receive guidance, support, and accountability. Wise mentors and fellow believers can offer valuable advice, share experiences, and provide encouragement along the journey. Hebrews 10:24-25 highlights the importance of community: "And let us consider one another to provoke unto love and to good works: Not forsaking the assembling of ourselves together, as the manner of some is; but exhorting one another: and so much the more, as ye see the day approaching." This sense of community helps believers stay on track, providing direction and support in their spiritual journey.

Direction in both hunting and the Christian life also involves a clear sense of purpose. Hunters embark on their journey with a specific goal in mind, whether it is to track a particular animal or to explore a new area. This sense of purpose keeps them focused and motivated, even when the path is challenging. Similarly, Christians are called to live with a sense of purpose, knowing that their ultimate goal is to glorify God and share His love with others. This purpose provides a clear direction, helping believers stay focused on their mission and navigate life's complexities with intentionality and conviction. Ephesians 2:10 says, "For we are his workmanship, created in Christ Jesus unto good works, which God hath before ordained that we should walk in them." This verse emphasizes that Christians are created with a purpose and are called to live out that purpose in their daily lives.

In both hunting and the Christian life, direction is often confirmed through experience and reflection. Hunters learn from each outing, reflecting on what worked and what did not, and adjusting their strategies accordingly. This reflective practice helps them improve their skills and become more effective in their pursuits. Similarly, Christians grow in their ability to discern God's direction through experience and reflection. By looking back on how God has guided them in the past, they can gain confidence and clarity for the future. This reflection helps them recognize God's hand in their lives and trust in His continued guidance. Psalm 77:11-12 says, "I will remember the works of the LORD: surely I will remember thy wonders of old. I will meditate also of all thy work, and talk of thy doings." This practice of reflection and meditation helps believers stay aligned with God's direction and appreciate His faithfulness.

Direction also involves a commitment to ethical and responsible behavior. Hunters must navigate their environment with respect for wildlife and the natural world, following regulations and ethical guidelines to ensure sustainable practices. This ethical approach is a key aspect of responsible hunting, reflecting a commitment to preserving the environment for future generations. Similarly, Christians are called to navigate their lives with integrity and ethical behavior, following God's commandments and living in a way that honors Him. This involves being honest, kind, and just in all interactions, striving to reflect Christ's character in every aspect of life. Micah 6:8 encapsulates this ethical call: "He hath shewed thee, O man, what is good; and what doth the LORD require of thee, but to do justly, and to love mercy, and to walk humbly with thy God?"

In conclusion, direction is a fundamental aspect of success and fulfillment in both hunting and the Christian life. For hunters, direction means having a clear sense of the path, utilizing tools and resources, and adapting to changing conditions to navigate the wilderness effectively. It involves preparation, patience, community support, and a commitment to ethical practices. For Christians, direction means seeking God's guidance in every aspect of life, relying on spiritual tools like the Bible and prayer, and remaining open to the leading of the Holy Spirit. It involves trusting in God's plans, persevering through challenges, and living with a sense of purpose and integrity. Psalm 32:8 encapsulates this divine guidance: "I will instruct thee and teach thee in the way which thou shalt go: I will guide thee with mine eye." By embracing the principles of direction in their respective pursuits, both hunters and Christians can achieve their goals, grow in their skills and faith, and live lives that honor God. Direction is a journey marked by continuous effort, learning, and a commitment to ethical behavior and integrity, leading to success and fulfillment in both hunting and the Christian life.

Chapter 8 Distance

Distance is a key element in both hunting and the Christian life, involving the careful balance of proximity and separation to achieve desired outcomes. For hunters, maintaining the correct distance from their prey is essential for a successful hunt. This involves knowing when to get closer and when to stay hidden, ensuring they do not startle the animal while positioning themselves for a clear shot. Hunters must be skilled in reading the environment and understanding the behavior of their prey to gauge the appropriate distance. They often use tools like binoculars to observe from afar and gradually close the gap with stealth and patience. This delicate balance requires acute awareness, precision, and self-control. A hunter who gets too close too quickly risks scaring away the game, while one who stays too far may miss the opportunity altogether. This careful management of distance underscores the hunter's respect for the natural world and their commitment to ethical hunting practices. It involves not only physical space but also a strategic understanding of timing and movement, ensuring that each step is calculated to maintain the element of surprise and effectiveness.

Similarly, in the Christian life, maintaining a spiritual distance from sin is crucial for living a life that honors God. Christians are called to be in the world but not of it, meaning they must navigate their daily lives without being drawn into behaviors and attitudes that contradict their faith. This involves making conscious choices to avoid situations, influences, and actions that can lead to sin. James 4:8 emphasizes the importance of drawing near to God and distancing oneself from sin: "Draw nigh to God, and he will draw nigh to you. Cleanse your hands, ye sinners; and purify your hearts, ye double minded." This verse encourages believers to seek closeness with God while actively resisting and separating themselves from sinful behaviors. Maintaining this spiritual distance involves regular self-examination, repentance, and a commitment to living according to God's word. By keeping a healthy distance from sin, Christians can protect their spiritual well-being and grow closer to God, experiencing His presence and guidance more fully.

For both hunters and Christians, distance involves a delicate balance that requires constant vigilance and intentionality. Hunters must continuously assess their surroundings and adjust their position to stay within an optimal range of their prey. This requires a deep understanding of animal behavior, environmental factors, and the use of tools and techniques to remain undetected. Similarly, Christians must remain aware of the influences and temptations around them, making conscious decisions to uphold their faith and integrity. This involves setting boundaries, avoiding compromising situations, and surrounding themselves with positive influences that encourage spiritual growth. By maintaining this careful balance, both hunters and Christians can navigate their respective paths with wisdom and effectiveness.

Distance also involves preparation and strategy. Hunters prepare by studying the habits and patterns of their prey, choosing the right equipment, and planning their approach to maintain the correct distance. This preparation ensures they can move efficiently and effectively, minimizing the risk of detection. Similarly, Christians prepare by immersing themselves in God's word, prayer, and fellowship with other believers. This spiritual preparation strengthens their faith and equips them to resist temptation and stay close to God. By grounding themselves in their faith, Christians can navigate life's challenges with clarity and purpose, maintaining a healthy distance from sin while drawing nearer to God.

Both hunters and Christians must also be adaptable, ready to adjust their distance based on changing circumstances. Hunters might need to quickly alter their position if the wind shifts, the terrain changes, or the prey behaves unexpectedly. This adaptability is crucial for maintaining the element of surprise and achieving success. Similarly,

Christians must be adaptable in their spiritual journey, remaining sensitive to the Holy Spirit's guidance and being willing to change course when necessary. Life is full of unexpected challenges and opportunities, and a rigid approach can lead to spiritual stagnation or compromise. By staying flexible and responsive to God's leading, Christians can maintain their spiritual integrity and continue to grow in their faith.

Patience and perseverance are also essential in managing distance effectively. Hunters often need to wait for long periods, remaining still and quiet to avoid alerting their prey. This patience is a testament to their dedication and discipline, ensuring they do not rush and risk losing their opportunity. Similarly, Christians are called to be patient and persevere in their faith, even when faced with trials and temptations. James 1:12 says, "Blessed is the man that endureth temptation: for when he is tried, he shall receive the crown of life, which the Lord hath promised to them that love him." This verse encourages believers to remain steadfast, trusting that their perseverance will be rewarded.

Community and support play a significant role in helping both hunters and Christians manage distance effectively. Hunters often share tips, techniques, and experiences with one another, creating a network of knowledge and encouragement. This sense of community enhances their skills and success. Similarly, Christians benefit from being part of a faith community where they can receive guidance, support, and accountability. Fellow believers can offer valuable advice, share experiences, and provide encouragement to help maintain spiritual distance from sin and draw closer to God. Hebrews 10:24-25 highlights the importance of this community: "And let us consider one another to provoke unto love and to good works: Not forsaking the assembling of ourselves together, as the manner of some is; but exhorting one another: and so much the more, as ye see the day approaching." This sense of community helps believers stay on track, providing direction and support in their spiritual journey.

Distance in both hunting and the Christian life also involves a commitment to ethical behavior and integrity. Hunters adhere to ethical hunting practices, ensuring that they respect wildlife and follow regulations. This integrity reflects their commitment to ethical principles and fosters a deeper respect for nature. Similarly, Christians are called to live with integrity, following God's commandments and reflecting their faith in their actions. This involves being honest, kind, and just in all interactions, striving to live a life that honors God. Micah 6:8 encapsulates this ethical call: "He hath shewed thee, O man, what is good; and what doth the LORD require of thee, but to do justly, and to love mercy, and to walk humbly with thy God?"

Reflection and learning are also crucial components of managing distance. Hunters reflect on their experiences, learning from each outing to improve their skills and strategies. This reflective practice helps them better understand how to maintain the correct distance and adapt to different scenarios. Similarly, Christians grow in their ability to discern the appropriate spiritual distance through reflection and learning. By looking back on their spiritual journey and considering how God has guided them, they can gain valuable insights and adjust their approach accordingly. This reflection helps them recognize areas where they need to create more distance from sin and draw closer to God. Psalm 119:105 says, "Thy word is a lamp unto my feet, and a light unto my path." This verse highlights the importance of regularly engaging with Scripture to illuminate one's path and maintain the right spiritual distance.

In conclusion, distance is a fundamental aspect of success and fulfillment in both hunting and the Christian life. For hunters, maintaining the correct distance from their prey involves a careful balance of proximity and separation, requiring knowledge, patience, adaptability, and ethical behavior. It involves strategic planning, preparation, and the ability to adjust to changing conditions to remain undetected and achieve success. For Christians, maintaining a spiritual distance from sin involves a conscious effort to uphold their faith and integrity while navigating the world. It requires regular self-examination, repentance, and a commitment to living according to God's word. James 4:8 encapsulates this call to draw near to God and maintain a distance from sin: "Draw nigh to God, and he will draw nigh to you. Cleanse your hands, ye sinners; and purify your hearts, ye double minded." By embracing the principles of distance in their respective pursuits, both hunters and Christians can achieve their goals, grow in their skills and faith, and live lives that honor God. Distance is a journey marked by continuous effort, learning, and a commitment to ethical behavior and integrity, leading to success and fulfillment in both hunting and the Christian life.

Chapter 9 Danger

Danger is a significant aspect in both hunting and the Christian life, as hunters encounter various inherent dangers from wildlife and the environment, and Christians face spiritual dangers and temptations. For hunters, venturing into the wilderness brings numerous risks, including encounters with dangerous animals such as bears, wolves, or snakes. These animals can pose a serious threat if provoked or if a hunter inadvertently gets too close. Additionally, the natural environment itself can be perilous, with hunters navigating through rugged terrains, dense forests, steep cliffs, and fast-flowing rivers. Weather conditions can change rapidly, bringing sudden storms, extreme temperatures, or heavy snowfall, all of which can create hazardous situations. Hunters must be prepared to face these dangers, equipped with the necessary gear, knowledge, and skills to handle emergencies. This includes carrying first aid kits, knowing how to navigate using a compass or GPS, and being trained in survival techniques. Hunters also need to be vigilant and aware of their surroundings, constantly assessing potential threats and making decisions that ensure their safety. The presence of firearms adds another layer of danger, requiring strict adherence to safety protocols to prevent accidents. The risks associated with hunting highlight the importance of preparation, caution, and respect for the natural world, emphasizing that hunting is not just a sport but a serious endeavor that demands responsibility and awareness.

Similarly, in the Christian life, believers face spiritual dangers and temptations that can threaten their faith and spiritual well-being. Christians are called to live in a world that often opposes their values and beliefs, and they must navigate through various challenges and temptations that can lead them away from God. These spiritual dangers include the temptation to sin, the influence of secular culture, and the subtle deceptions of false teachings. The Bible warns believers to be vigilant and to guard their hearts and minds against these threats.

Ephesians 6:11 emphasizes the need for spiritual preparedness: "Put on the whole armour of God, that ye may be able to stand against the wiles of the devil." This verse encourages Christians to equip themselves with spiritual armor, including truth, righteousness, faith, salvation, the Word of God, and prayer, to withstand the attacks and deceptions of the enemy. Just as hunters must prepare and protect themselves from physical dangers, Christians must prepare and protect themselves from spiritual dangers by grounding themselves in God's Word, maintaining a strong prayer life, and staying connected to a supportive faith community.

For both hunters and Christians, danger requires a proactive and vigilant approach. Hunters must always be aware of their surroundings, anticipating potential threats and taking measures to avoid or mitigate them. This might involve choosing safe hunting locations, avoiding areas known for dangerous wildlife, and traveling in groups for added safety. Similarly, Christians must be vigilant in their spiritual walk, recognizing the subtle ways in which temptations and spiritual dangers can infiltrate their lives. This vigilance involves regular self-examination, seeking accountability from fellow believers, and being discerning about the influences they allow into their lives. By staying alert and proactive, both hunters and Christians can better navigate the dangers they face and maintain their focus on their goals.

Preparation is another key aspect of managing danger. Hunters prepare by ensuring they have the right equipment, knowledge, and skills to handle emergencies and unexpected situations. This preparation might include taking survival courses, learning first aid, and practicing safety protocols with firearms. Similarly, Christians prepare for spiritual dangers by immersing themselves in Scripture, prayer, and fellowship with other believers. This spiritual preparation strengthens their faith and equips them to recognize and resist temptations. By grounding themselves in God's truth and staying connected to a supportive community, Christians can better withstand the spiritual dangers they encounter.

Adaptability is also crucial when facing danger. Hunters must be able to adapt to changing conditions, such as sudden weather changes or unexpected wildlife encounters. This adaptability involves staying calm, making quick decisions, and using available resources to ensure safety. Similarly, Christians must be adaptable in their spiritual journey, remaining flexible and responsive to God's guidance. Life is full of unexpected challenges, and a rigid approach can leave believers vulnerable to spiritual attacks. By staying adaptable and trusting in God's sovereignty, Christians can navigate spiritual dangers with resilience and faith.

Both hunters and Christians benefit from a community that provides support and guidance in times of danger. Hunters often rely on the knowledge and experience of more seasoned hunters, learning from their wisdom and following their advice to stay safe. This sense of community enhances their ability to handle dangerous situations effectively. Similarly, Christians are part of a faith community that offers support, encouragement, and accountability. Fellow believers can provide valuable insights, share experiences, and pray for one another, helping to strengthen their resolve and protect against spiritual dangers. Hebrews 10:24-25 highlights the importance of this community: "And let us consider one another to provoke unto love and to good works: Not forsaking the assembling of ourselves together, as the manner of some is; but exhorting one another: and so much the more, as ye see the day approaching."

Courage is another essential quality when facing danger. Hunters must be courageous, willing to venture into the wilderness despite the risks, and face potential threats with confidence and determination. This courage is built through experience, preparation, and a deep respect for nature. Similarly, Christians are called to be courageous in their faith, standing firm against spiritual dangers and trusting in

God's protection. Joshua 1:9 encourages believers to be strong and courageous: "Have not I commanded thee? Be strong and of a good courage; be not afraid, neither be thou dismayed: for the LORD thy God is with thee whithersoever thou goest." This courage is rooted in the assurance of God's presence and His promises, giving believers the confidence to face any spiritual challenge.

Ethical behavior and integrity are also important in managing danger. Hunters must adhere to ethical hunting practices, respecting wildlife and the environment, and following safety protocols to prevent accidents. This ethical approach reflects a commitment to responsible hunting and a respect for the natural world. Similarly, Christians are called to live with integrity, following God's commandments and reflecting their faith in their actions. This involves being honest, kind, and just in all interactions, striving to live a life that honors God. Micah 6:8 encapsulates this ethical call: "He hath shewed thee, O man, what is good; and what doth the LORD require of thee, but to do justly, and to love mercy, and to walk humbly with thy God?"

Both hunters and Christians can learn and grow from their experiences with danger. Hunters reflect on their encounters with danger, learning from each experience to improve their skills and strategies. This reflective practice helps them better understand how to manage risks and make safer decisions in the future. Similarly, Christians grow in their ability to recognize and resist spiritual dangers through reflection and learning. By looking back on their spiritual journey and considering how God has guided and protected them, they can gain valuable insights and strengthen their faith. This reflection helps them recognize areas where they need to be more vigilant and committed to living according to God's Word.

In conclusion, danger is an integral part of both hunting and the Christian life, requiring careful management, preparation, and a proactive approach. Hunters face inherent dangers from wildlife and the environment, requiring them to be vigilant, prepared, and adaptable. They rely on their skills, knowledge, and the support of their community to navigate these risks effectively. Similarly, Christians face spiritual dangers and temptations that can threaten their faith and well-being. They are called to put on the whole armor of God, grounding themselves in Scripture, prayer, and fellowship to withstand the attacks of the enemy. Ephesians 6:11 emphasizes the importance of this spiritual preparedness: "Put on the whole armour of God, that ye may be able to stand against the wiles of the devil." By embracing the principles of managing danger in their respective pursuits, both hunters and Christians can achieve their goals, grow in their skills and faith, and live lives that honor God. Danger is a journey marked by continuous effort, learning, and a commitment to ethical behavior and integrity, leading to success and fulfillment in both hunting and the Christian life.

Chapter 10 Discernment

Discernment is a crucial quality in both hunting and the Christian life, requiring the ability to accurately identify targets and make wise decisions. For hunters, discernment means being able to accurately identify their target, distinguishing between different animals, and making sure they have a clear and ethical shot. This involves a deep understanding of wildlife, knowing the specific characteristics of the animals they are hunting, and being able to spot the subtle differences that distinguish one species from another. Hunters need to be aware of the laws and regulations that protect certain species and ensure they do not mistakenly target the wrong animal. This discernment is essential for ethical hunting, ensuring that hunters respect wildlife and contribute to conservation efforts. Hunters also need to discern the best times and places to hunt, taking into account factors such as animal behavior, weather conditions, and terrain. This requires careful observation, experience, and a keen awareness of the natural environment. The ability to discern the right moment to take a shot is critical, as a hasty or ill-judged decision can lead to missed opportunities or unethical outcomes. Hunters often rely on their senses, such as sight and hearing, as well as their knowledge and experience, to make these discerning decisions. They must be patient and wait for the right moment, understanding that successful hunting is not just about taking a shot but about making the right choices throughout the entire process.

Similarly, in the Christian life, discernment is essential for making wise spiritual decisions and living a life that aligns with God's will. Christians need spiritual discernment to distinguish between what is true and what is false, to recognize God's voice, and to identify the influences and teachings that align with biblical truth. This discernment helps believers navigate a world filled with conflicting messages, temptations, and false teachings. 1 John 4:1 highlights the importance of discernment: "Beloved, believe not every spirit, but try the spirits whether they are of God." This verse encourages Christians to test the spirits and to discern whether they are from God, emphasizing the need for vigilance and wisdom in their spiritual journey. Spiritual discernment involves a deep understanding of Scripture, a strong relationship with God, and the guidance of the Holy Spirit. By grounding themselves in God's Word and seeking His wisdom, Christians can develop the discernment needed to make choices that honor Him and reflect His truth.

For both hunters and Christians, discernment requires a combination of knowledge, experience, and intuition. Hunters gain discernment through years of practice and observation, learning to recognize the signs and behaviors that indicate the presence of their target. This knowledge is built over time and is often shared within the hunting community, with more experienced hunters passing on their insights to novices. Similarly, Christians develop spiritual discernment through regular study of the Bible, prayer, and fellowship with other believers. This ongoing spiritual practice helps them grow in their understanding of God's truth and equips them to recognize false teachings and influences. By immersing themselves in Scripture and seeking God's guidance, Christians can sharpen their discernment and make wise decisions in their daily lives.

Discernment also involves the ability to make quick and accurate judgments in the moment. Hunters must be able to assess a situation rapidly, determining whether it is safe and ethical to take a shot. This split-second decision-making requires confidence and clarity, as well as a deep trust in their knowledge and skills. Similarly, Christians often face situations where they must make quick decisions based on their spiritual discernment. This might involve choosing how to respond to a challenging situation, determining whether an opportunity aligns with God's will, or recognizing and resisting temptation. By staying attuned to the Holy Spirit and relying on their understanding of Scripture,

Christians can make discerning choices that honor God and reflect their faith.

Both hunters and Christians benefit from the guidance and support of their communities in developing discernment. Hunters often learn from more experienced hunters, gaining insights and tips that help them make better decisions in the field. This sense of community and shared knowledge enhances their ability to discern and succeed. Similarly, Christians are part of a faith community that provides support, encouragement, and accountability. Fellow believers can offer wisdom, share their experiences, and pray for one another, helping to strengthen their discernment and spiritual growth. Hebrews 10:24-25 highlights the importance of this community: "And let us consider one another to provoke unto love and to good works: Not forsaking the assembling of ourselves together, as the manner of some is; but exhorting one another: and so much the more, as ye see the day approaching." This sense of community helps believers stay grounded in their faith and grow in their ability to discern God's truth.

Preparation is another key aspect of discernment. Hunters prepare by studying their prey, understanding their behavior, and practicing their skills to ensure they can make accurate and ethical shots. This preparation helps them develop the discernment needed to identify their target and make wise decisions in the field. Similarly, Christians prepare for spiritual discernment by immersing themselves in God's Word, spending time in prayer, and seeking the guidance of the Holy Spirit. This spiritual preparation equips them to recognize and respond to the challenges and opportunities they encounter, helping them to live according to God's will.

Patience and perseverance are also essential components of discernment. Hunters often need to wait for the right moment to take a shot, demonstrating patience and self-control. This patience allows them to make discerning decisions and avoid hasty or unethical actions. Similarly, Christians are called to be patient and persevere in their faith, trusting that God will provide the wisdom and guidance they need. James 1:5 encourages believers to seek God's wisdom: "If any of you lack wisdom, let him ask of God, that giveth to all men liberally, and upbraideth not; and it shall be given him." This verse reminds Christians that God is the source of all wisdom and that they can rely on Him for discernment in every situation.

Both hunters and Christians must also be aware of the potential for deception and falsehood. Hunters need to be cautious of misidentifying their target or being misled by their surroundings. This awareness helps them stay focused and make accurate decisions. Similarly, Christians must be vigilant in discerning between true and false teachings, recognizing that not everything they encounter will align with God's truth. This vigilance involves testing the spirits, as 1 John 4:1 instructs, and being discerning about the influences they allow into their lives.

Reflection and learning from experiences are crucial for developing discernment. Hunters reflect on their successes and mistakes, learning from each experience to improve their skills and judgment. This reflective practice helps them become more discerning and effective in their pursuits. Similarly, Christians grow in their ability to discern through reflection and learning. By looking back on their spiritual journey and considering how God has guided them, they can gain valuable insights and strengthen their faith. This reflection helps them recognize areas where they need to be more discerning and committed to living according to God's Word.

In conclusion, discernment is a fundamental aspect of success and fulfillment in both hunting and the Christian life. For hunters, discernment means accurately identifying their target, making ethical decisions, and navigating the challenges of the natural environment. It involves a combination of knowledge, experience, intuition, and preparation, as well as the guidance and support of the hunting community. For Christians, discernment means distinguishing between truth and falsehood, recognizing God's voice, and making decisions that align with His will. It involves regular study of Scripture, prayer, and fellowship with other believers, as well as a deep reliance on the Holy Spirit. 1 John 4:1 encapsulates this call to spiritual discernment: "Beloved, believe not every spirit, but try the spirits whether they are of God." By embracing the principles of discernment in their respective pursuits, both hunters and Christians can achieve their goals, grow in their skills and faith, and live lives that honor God. Discernment is a journey marked by continuous effort, learning, and a commitment to ethical behavior and integrity, leading to success and fulfillment in both hunting and the Christian life.

Chapter 11 Diet

Diet plays a crucial role in both hunting and the Christian life, emphasizing the importance of sustenance and nourishment for physical and spiritual well-being. For hunters, maintaining a specific diet in the wild is essential for survival and peak performance. When out in the wilderness, hunters often have to rely on what they can carry or find, making it necessary to plan and prepare their food supplies carefully. This might include non-perishable items like jerky, nuts, dried fruits, and energy bars, which provide the necessary nutrients and energy to sustain them during long hunts. Hunters also need to be knowledgeable about foraging, identifying edible plants, and understanding which parts of the animal they can safely consume if they hunt for their food. This diet is not just about survival but also about maintaining the strength, endurance, and focus needed for successful hunting. Proper nutrition ensures that hunters can stay alert, make good decisions, and have the stamina to track and hunt their prey. This careful planning and understanding of their dietary needs underscore the hunter's preparation and adaptability, highlighting the importance of diet in their overall strategy and success.

Similarly, in the Christian life, diet takes on a spiritual dimension, emphasizing the importance of feeding on the Word of God for spiritual nourishment and growth. Christians are called to live not by physical bread alone but by every word that comes from the mouth of God, as stated in Matthew 4:4: "Man shall not live by bread alone, but by every word that proceedeth out of the mouth of God." This verse underscores the importance of Scripture as the primary source of spiritual sustenance. Just as physical food nourishes the body, the Word of God nourishes the soul, providing the wisdom, guidance, and strength needed to navigate the challenges of life. Regular reading, studying, and meditating on the Bible are essential practices for Christians to grow in their faith and stay spiritually healthy. The Bible offers teachings, commandments, and stories that inspire, correct, and guide believers, helping them align their lives with God's will and purpose.

For both hunters and Christians, diet involves careful selection and preparation. Hunters must choose foods that are lightweight, nutritious, and easy to carry, ensuring they have enough energy to sustain them during their hunts. This preparation involves planning their meals, understanding their nutritional needs, and making sure they have access to clean water and safe food sources in the wild. Similarly, Christians must be intentional about their spiritual diet, choosing to immerse themselves in Scripture and avoid teachings or influences that could lead them astray. This involves regular Bible reading, participating in Bible studies, and seeking out sound doctrine and teachings that align with the truths of the faith. By being intentional about their spiritual diet, Christians can ensure they are feeding on the pure and nourishing Word of God, which helps them grow stronger in their faith and better equipped to face spiritual challenges.

Discipline is another critical aspect of maintaining a proper diet. Hunters need to have the discipline to stick to their food supplies and ration their provisions wisely, especially during extended hunts. This discipline ensures that they do not run out of food and can maintain their energy levels throughout their time in the wild. Similarly, Christians need to be disciplined in their spiritual practices, consistently feeding on the Word of God and maintaining a regular devotional life. This discipline helps them stay spiritually healthy and focused on their relationship with God, avoiding spiritual malnutrition that can occur when they neglect their time with God's Word.

Both hunters and Christians also benefit from the support and knowledge of their communities in maintaining their diets. Hunters often share tips and techniques for foraging, preparing, and preserving food, creating a network of shared knowledge that enhances their ability to sustain themselves in the wild. This community support is invaluable, providing practical advice and encouragement. Similarly, Christians benefit from being part of a faith community that encourages and supports their spiritual growth. Fellow believers can share insights from Scripture, offer accountability, and pray for one another, helping to ensure that everyone stays nourished by the Word of God. Hebrews 10:24-25 emphasizes the importance of this community support: "And let us consider one another to provoke unto love and to good works: Not forsaking the assembling of ourselves together, as the manner of some is; but exhorting one another: and so much the more, as ye see the day approaching." This sense of community helps believers stay committed to their spiritual diet and grow in their faith.

Adaptability is also crucial when it comes to diet. Hunters need to be adaptable in their food choices, sometimes relying on what is available in their environment. This might mean learning to identify and prepare wild edibles or adjusting their diet based on the game they hunt. This adaptability ensures that they can sustain themselves regardless of the conditions they face. Similarly, Christians need to be adaptable in their spiritual diet, being open to different ways of engaging with Scripture and learning from diverse sources. This might involve reading different translations of the Bible, participating in various Bible study groups, or exploring different devotional practices. By staying adaptable, Christians can continue to grow and deepen their understanding of God's Word, finding new and enriching ways to nourish their spiritual lives.

Reflection and learning from experience are also important components of maintaining a proper diet. Hunters reflect on their experiences, learning what food sources are most effective and how to better prepare for future hunts. This reflection helps them improve their diet and overall strategy, ensuring they are better equipped for the challenges they face. Similarly, Christians grow in their ability to feed on the Word of God through reflection and learning. By considering how God's Word has nourished and guided them in the past, they can gain insights and make adjustments to their spiritual practices. This reflection helps them recognize the importance of staying committed to their spiritual diet and finding new ways to engage with Scripture. Psalm 119:105 says, "Thy word is a lamp unto my feet, and a light unto my path." This verse highlights the importance of regularly engaging with Scripture to illuminate one's path and maintain spiritual nourishment.

Both hunters and Christians must also be mindful of the quality of their diet. Hunters need to ensure that their food is safe to eat and provides the necessary nutrients. This involves being cautious about what they forage and how they prepare and store their food. Similarly, Christians need to be discerning about the teachings and influences they consume, ensuring they align with biblical truth. This discernment involves testing the spirits, as 1 John 4:1 instructs, and being careful about the sources of their spiritual nourishment. By maintaining a high-quality diet, both physically and spiritually, hunters and Christians can ensure they are well-nourished and healthy.

In conclusion, diet is a fundamental aspect of both hunting and the Christian life, emphasizing the importance of sustenance and nourishment for physical and spiritual well-being. For hunters, maintaining a specific diet in the wild involves careful planning, preparation, and adaptability, ensuring they have the energy and strength needed for successful hunting. It requires discipline, community support, and the ability to learn and adapt based on experience. For Christians, diet takes on a spiritual dimension, emphasizing the importance of feeding on the Word of God for spiritual nourishment and growth. This involves regular Bible reading, studying, and meditating on Scripture, maintaining discipline in their spiritual practices, and being part of a supportive faith community. Matthew 4:4 encapsulates this call to spiritual nourishment: "Man shall not live by bread alone, but by every word that proceedeth out of the mouth of God." By embracing the principles of maintaining a proper diet in their respective pursuits, both hunters and Christians can achieve their goals, grow in their skills and faith, and live lives that honor God. Diet is a journey marked by continuous effort, learning, and a commitment to nourishment and well-being, leading to success and fulfillment in both hunting and the Christian life.

Chapter 12 Doubt

Doubt is a significant challenge in both hunting and the Christian life, and overcoming it is crucial for success and fulfillment. In hunting, doubt can creep in at various stages, whether it's questioning one's skills, the chosen hunting spot, or the chances of success. Hunters must overcome these doubts to make decisive actions, such as taking a shot or making strategic decisions about where to position themselves. Doubt can lead to hesitation, which in turn can result in missed opportunities or even dangerous situations if one second-guesses critical safety measures. To overcome doubt, hunters rely on their training, experience, and instincts. Preparation is key; knowing their equipment is in top condition, understanding the behavior of their prey, and being familiar with the terrain all help to build confidence. Hunters also learn to trust their instincts, developed through hours of practice and observation. When a hunter has confidence in their abilities and their preparation, they are better equipped to make quick, decisive actions when the moment arises. This ability to push through doubt and act decisively is essential for a successful hunt. It also involves a mental toughness, a belief in oneself, and a willingness to take calculated risks based on knowledge and experience. Overcoming doubt in hunting is not about being free from fear but about acknowledging it and moving forward with determination and focus.

Similarly, in the Christian life, doubt can be a significant obstacle that believers must overcome to live a life of faith. Doubts about God's presence, His promises, or one's own faith can lead to spiritual stagnation or even despair. Christians are called to overcome these doubts with faith, trusting in God's word and His promises. Mark 11:23 highlights the power of faith in overcoming doubt: "For verily I say unto you, That whosoever shall say unto this mountain, Be thou removed, and be thou cast into the sea; and shall not doubt in his heart, but shall believe that those things which he saith shall come to pass;

he shall have whatsoever he saith." This verse emphasizes that faith can move mountains, a powerful metaphor for overcoming the obstacles and doubts that believers face. Faith is built through a relationship with God, regular prayer, and studying the Bible. By immersing themselves in Scripture, Christians are reminded of God's faithfulness and His promises, which helps to strengthen their faith and dispel doubt. Prayer is another vital tool in overcoming doubt, as it allows believers to communicate with God, express their concerns, and seek His guidance and reassurance. Through prayer, Christians can find peace and confidence, knowing that God hears their prayers and is with them in their struggles.

For both hunters and Christians, overcoming doubt requires a combination of preparation, experience, and trust. Hunters prepare by honing their skills, studying their environment, and ensuring their equipment is ready. This preparation helps to build confidence and reduce doubt. Similarly, Christians prepare by deepening their understanding of God's word, participating in worship, and seeking fellowship with other believers. This spiritual preparation equips them to face doubts with faith and resilience. Experience also plays a crucial role in overcoming doubt. Hunters gain confidence through each successful hunt and learn from their mistakes, gradually reducing doubt and increasing their decisiveness. Similarly, Christians grow in their faith through experiences of God's faithfulness and answered prayers. Each time they see God's hand at work in their lives, their faith is strengthened, and their doubts diminish. Trust is another essential component. Hunters must trust in their skills, their preparation, and their instincts. This trust allows them to act decisively even when doubt tries to creep in. Similarly, Christians must trust in God's promises and His character. Trusting that God is good, that He loves them, and that He has a plan for their lives helps believers to overcome doubt and live confidently in their faith.

Both hunters and Christians also benefit from the support and encouragement of their communities in overcoming doubt. Hunters often rely on the wisdom and experience of more seasoned hunters, learning from their successes and failures. This mentorship and camaraderie provide valuable insights and encouragement, helping to build confidence and reduce doubt. Similarly, Christians are part of a faith community that offers support, encouragement, and accountability. Fellow believers can share their own experiences of overcoming doubt, provide reassurance, and pray for one another. Hebrews 10:24-25 emphasizes the importance of this community support: "And let us consider one another to provoke unto love and to good works: Not forsaking the assembling of ourselves together, as the manner of some is; but exhorting one another: and so much the more, as ye see the day approaching." This sense of community helps believers to stay strong in their faith and overcome doubts.

Reflection and learning from experiences are also crucial for overcoming doubt. Hunters reflect on their experiences, analyzing what worked and what didn't, and applying these lessons to future hunts. This reflective practice helps to build confidence and reduce doubt over time. Similarly, Christians grow in their faith by reflecting on their spiritual journey and recognizing God's faithfulness in their lives. By considering how God has guided and provided for them in the past, they can gain confidence and trust for the future. This reflection helps to strengthen their faith and dispel doubt.

Overcoming doubt also involves a commitment to continuous learning and growth. Hunters continually seek to improve their skills and knowledge, staying up to date with new techniques and information. This commitment to learning helps them to stay confident and reduce doubt. Similarly, Christians are called to continually grow in their faith, seeking to know God more deeply and understand His word more fully. This involves regular Bible study, prayer, and engaging with sound teaching. By continually seeking to grow in their faith, Christians can strengthen their trust in God and overcome doubts.

Adaptability is another important aspect of overcoming doubt. Hunters must be adaptable, ready to adjust their plans and strategies based on changing conditions. This flexibility helps them to remain confident and decisive even when faced with unexpected challenges. Similarly, Christians must be adaptable in their spiritual journey, remaining open to God's leading and willing to adjust their plans according to His will. Life is full of unexpected challenges, and a rigid approach can lead to increased doubt and frustration. By staying flexible and trusting in God's guidance, Christians can navigate these challenges with confidence and faith.

Both hunters and Christians must also be aware of the potential for external influences to amplify their doubts. Hunters need to stay focused and avoid distractions that can lead to hesitation and doubt. This might involve tuning out negative voices or staying focused on their goals despite challenging conditions. Similarly, Christians must be vigilant about the influences they allow into their lives, recognizing that negative or misleading messages can increase doubt. This vigilance involves testing the spirits, as 1 John 4:1 instructs, and being discerning about the sources of their spiritual nourishment. By maintaining a focus on God's truth and avoiding negative influences, both hunters and Christians can reduce doubt and stay confident in their path.

In conclusion, doubt is a significant challenge in both hunting and the Christian life, but it can be overcome through preparation, experience, trust, community support, reflection, learning, and adaptability. Hunters must overcome doubt to make decisive actions, relying on their training, instincts, and the support of their community. Similarly, Christians are called to overcome doubt with faith, trusting in God's promises and seeking His guidance through prayer and Scripture. Mark 11:23 encapsulates this call to faith: "For verily I say unto you, That whosoever shall say unto this mountain, Be thou removed, and be thou cast into the sea; and shall not doubt in his heart, but shall believe that those things which he saith shall come to pass; he shall have whatsoever he saith." By embracing the principles of overcoming doubt in their respective pursuits, both hunters and Christians can achieve their goals, grow in their skills and faith, and live lives that honor God. Overcoming doubt is a journey marked by continuous effort, learning, and a commitment to confidence and faith, leading to success and fulfillment in both hunting and the Christian life.

Chapter 13 Direction

Direction is crucial for both hunting and the Christian life, requiring careful consideration, guidance, and adaptability to achieve success. In hunting, choosing the right direction is vital for a successful hunt. Hunters need to have a clear understanding of the terrain, the habits and patterns of their prey, and the best routes to take to position themselves advantageously. This involves extensive preparation, including studying maps, tracking signs, and sometimes even using GPS technology to navigate unfamiliar areas. Hunters must be able to read the environment, noticing subtle changes in the wind, weather, and animal behavior, and adjust their course accordingly. A hunter who sets out in the wrong direction risks not only missing their target but also encountering unnecessary dangers, such as getting lost or facing difficult terrain. Successful hunters rely on their experience, knowledge, and intuition to choose the right path, often consulting with fellow hunters and learning from past experiences to improve their decision-making. This process of choosing the right direction involves a combination of planning, observation, and adaptability, ensuring that they can respond to changing conditions and stay focused on their goal. Whether it's moving stealthily through a dense forest, navigating a rugged mountain, or setting up in a strategic location, hunters must be constantly aware of their direction and ready to make adjustments as needed.

Similarly, in the Christian life, direction is essential for living according to God's will and fulfilling one's purpose. Christians seek God's direction through prayer, reading the Bible, and listening to the Holy Spirit. Proverbs 16:9 emphasizes the importance of divine guidance: "A man's heart deviseth his way: but the LORD directeth his steps." This verse highlights the idea that while people may plan their paths, it is ultimately God who guides their steps. Christians believe that God has a plan for each person and that seeking His direction helps them align their lives with His will. This involves being open to God's leading, even when it means changing plans or stepping out in faith. Just as hunters must read the signs in nature, Christians must be attentive to the ways God communicates with them, through Scripture, circumstances, and the counsel of other believers. By seeking God's direction, Christians can navigate the challenges and opportunities of life with confidence and purpose, trusting that He will guide them along the right path.

For both hunters and Christians, direction requires preparation and intentionality. Hunters prepare by studying their environment, practicing their skills, and planning their routes. This preparation helps them to navigate effectively and make informed decisions in the field. Similarly, Christians prepare by immersing themselves in God's Word, spending time in prayer, and seeking fellowship with other believers. This spiritual preparation equips them to discern God's direction and respond to His leading. By grounding themselves in their faith and remaining attentive to God's guidance, Christians can navigate life's challenges with clarity and assurance.

Adaptability is another crucial aspect of maintaining the right direction. Hunters must be able to adapt to changing conditions, such as shifting wind patterns, unexpected weather, or the sudden movement of their prey. This flexibility allows them to stay on course and adjust their strategies as needed. Similarly, Christians must be adaptable in their spiritual journey, remaining open to God's leading and willing to change course when necessary. Life is full of unexpected twists and turns, and a rigid approach can lead to frustration and missed opportunities. By staying flexible and trusting in God's sovereignty, Christians can navigate these changes with confidence and faith.

Patience and perseverance are also essential components of maintaining the right direction. Hunters often need to wait for long periods, remaining still and patient, to avoid alerting their prey and to seize the right moment for action. This patience is a testament to their dedication and discipline, ensuring they do not rush and risk losing their opportunity. Similarly, Christians are called to be patient and persevere in their faith, trusting that God will provide the wisdom and guidance they need. James 1:5 encourages believers to seek God's wisdom: "If any of you lack wisdom, let him ask of God, that giveth to all men liberally, and upbraideth not; and it shall be given him." This verse reminds Christians that God is the source of all wisdom and that they can rely on Him for direction in every situation.

Both hunters and Christians benefit from the support and guidance of their communities in maintaining the right direction. Hunters often learn from more experienced hunters, gaining insights and tips that help them make better decisions in the field. This sense of community and shared knowledge enhances their ability to navigate effectively and succeed. Similarly, Christians are part of a faith community that provides support, encouragement, and accountability. Fellow believers can offer wisdom, share their experiences, and pray for one another, helping to strengthen their resolve and keep them on the right path. Hebrews 10:24-25 highlights the importance of this community support: "And let us consider one another to provoke unto love and to good works: Not forsaking the assembling of ourselves together, as the manner of some is; but exhorting one another: and so much the more, as ye see the day approaching." This sense of community helps believers stay grounded in their faith and grow in their ability to discern God's direction.

Reflection and learning from experiences are crucial for maintaining the right direction. Hunters reflect on their experiences, analyzing what worked and what didn't, and applying these lessons to future hunts. This reflective practice helps them improve their skills and decision-making, ensuring they are better equipped for future challenges. Similarly, Christians grow in their ability to discern God's direction through reflection and learning. By looking back on their spiritual journey and considering how God has guided them, they can gain valuable insights and strengthen their faith. This reflection helps them recognize areas where they need to be more attentive to God's leading and committed to living according to His will. Psalm 119:105 says, "Thy word is a lamp unto my feet, and a light unto my path." This verse highlights the importance of regularly engaging with Scripture to illuminate one's path and maintain the right spiritual direction.

Both hunters and Christians must also be aware of the potential for distractions and obstacles that can lead them off course. Hunters need to stay focused and avoid distractions that can cause them to lose sight of their target or miss important signs in the environment. This might involve tuning out negative voices or staying focused on their goals despite challenging conditions. Similarly, Christians must be vigilant about the influences they allow into their lives, recognizing that distractions and negative influences can lead them away from God's path. This vigilance involves testing the spirits, as 1 John 4:1 instructs, and being discerning about the sources of their spiritual nourishment. By maintaining a focus on God's truth and avoiding distractions, both hunters and Christians can stay on course and achieve their goals.

In conclusion, direction is a fundamental aspect of success and fulfillment in both hunting and the Christian life. For hunters, maintaining the right direction involves careful planning, preparation, and adaptability, ensuring they can navigate the challenges of the natural environment and position themselves for success. It requires patience, perseverance, and the support of a knowledgeable community. For Christians, direction means seeking God's guidance and aligning their lives with His will. It involves regular study of Scripture, prayer, and fellowship with other believers, as well as a deep reliance on the Holy Spirit. Proverbs 16:9 encapsulates this call to divine guidance: "A man's heart deviseth his way: but the LORD directeth his steps." By embracing the principles of maintaining the right direction in their respective pursuits, both hunters and Christians can achieve their goals, grow in their skills and faith, and live lives that honor God. Direction is a journey marked by continuous effort, learning, and a commitment to following the right path, leading to success and fulfillment in both hunting and the Christian life.

Chapter 15 Desire

Desire plays a crucial role in both hunting and the Christian life, driving individuals to pursue their goals with passion and dedication. For hunters, a strong desire to succeed is essential for enduring the challenges and uncertainties of the hunt. This desire motivates hunters to wake up early, brave harsh weather conditions, and spend long hours in the wilderness. It fuels their determination to improve their skills, learn about their prey, and strategize their approach. Without a strong desire, the physical and mental demands of hunting would be overwhelming. This desire is not just about the thrill of the hunt, but also about a deep respect for nature and the satisfaction of mastering a challenging skill. Hunters who are passionate about their pursuit are more likely to put in the necessary effort to prepare and persevere, knowing that success is not guaranteed but is highly rewarding when achieved. They study animal behavior, practice their marksmanship, and refine their techniques, all driven by a desire to be the best they can be. This passion also fosters a sense of community among hunters, who share tips, stories, and support, further fueling their collective desire to succeed.

Similarly, in the Christian life, desire is fundamental to seeking and growing closer to God. Christians are called to desire a relationship with God, to seek Him with all their hearts, and to delight in His presence. Psalm 37:4 encapsulates this idea: "Delight thyself also in the LORD; and he shall give thee the desires of thine heart." This verse highlights the importance of aligning one's desires with God's will and finding joy in His presence. When Christians delight in God, their desires become more aligned with His purposes, and they experience fulfillment and peace. This desire drives believers to spend time in prayer, read the Bible, and participate in worship and fellowship. It encourages them to grow in their faith, serve others, and live out the teachings of Christ. Just as hunters are motivated by their passion for the hunt, Christians are motivated by their love for God and their desire to know Him more deeply. This desire helps them to persevere through trials, remain steadfast in their faith, and seek God's guidance in all aspects of life.

For both hunters and Christians, desire involves a deep commitment and dedication to their pursuits. Hunters commit to the rigorous demands of hunting, often planning trips months in advance, investing in quality gear, and practicing their skills regularly. This commitment is driven by a desire to succeed and a love for the hunt. Similarly, Christians commit to their spiritual journey, dedicating time and energy to grow in their faith and live according to God's will. This commitment involves regular participation in church activities, personal Bible study, and serving others. By nurturing their desire for God, Christians find the strength and motivation to overcome obstacles and stay faithful in their walk with Him.

Desire also requires perseverance and resilience. Hunters face numerous challenges, such as harsh weather, difficult terrain, and elusive prey. Their desire to succeed helps them to persevere through these challenges, learning from each experience and continually striving to improve. Similarly, Christians face spiritual challenges, including temptations, doubts, and trials. Their desire to seek God and grow in their faith helps them to persevere, trusting in God's promises and relying on His strength. James 1:12 says, "Blessed is the man that endureth temptation: for when he is tried, he shall receive the crown of life, which the Lord hath promised to them that love him." This verse encourages believers to remain steadfast in their faith, knowing that their desire to seek God will be rewarded.

Both hunters and Christians benefit from the support and encouragement of their communities in nurturing their desires. Hunters often share their passion with fellow hunters, forming bonds and learning from each other's experiences. This sense of community enhances their desire to succeed, providing motivation and support.

Similarly, Christians are part of a faith community that offers encouragement, accountability, and fellowship. Fellow believers can share insights, provide spiritual support, and pray for one another, helping to strengthen their collective desire to seek God. Hebrews 10:24-25 highlights the importance of this community support: "And let us consider one another to provoke unto love and to good works: Not forsaking the assembling of ourselves together, as the manner of some is; but exhorting one another: and so much the more, as ye see the day approaching." This sense of community helps believers to stay focused on their spiritual goals and grow in their desire for God.

Preparation is another key aspect of desire. Hunters prepare by studying their prey, practicing their skills, and planning their hunts. This preparation is driven by a desire to be successful and to respect the art of hunting. Similarly, Christians prepare by immersing themselves in God's Word, spending time in prayer, and seeking to understand God's will. This spiritual preparation is motivated by a desire to know God more intimately and to live according to His purposes. By being intentional about their preparation, both hunters and Christians can ensure they are well-equipped to pursue their goals and overcome challenges.

Desire also involves setting goals and striving for excellence. Hunters set goals for their hunts, such as tracking a specific animal or mastering a particular skill. These goals provide direction and motivation, helping them to stay focused and work diligently toward their objectives. Similarly, Christians set spiritual goals, such as deepening their prayer life, growing in their understanding of Scripture, or serving in their community. These goals help believers to stay focused on their spiritual journey and continually seek to grow in their faith. Philippians 3:14 says, "I press toward the mark for the prize of the high calling of God in Christ Jesus." This verse highlights the importance of setting spiritual goals and striving for excellence in one's faith.

Adaptability is another important aspect of desire. Hunters must be adaptable, ready to adjust their plans based on changing conditions, such as weather, terrain, or animal behavior. This flexibility allows them to stay focused on their goals and respond effectively to challenges. Similarly, Christians must be adaptable in their spiritual journey, remaining open to God's leading and willing to change course when necessary. Life is full of unexpected twists and turns, and a rigid approach can lead to frustration and missed opportunities. By staying flexible and trusting in God's guidance, Christians can navigate these changes with confidence and faith.

Reflection and learning from experiences are also crucial for nurturing desire. Hunters reflect on their successes and failures, learning from each experience to improve their skills and strategies. This reflective practice helps them to grow in their passion for hunting and their desire to succeed. Similarly, Christians grow in their faith by reflecting on their spiritual journey and recognizing God's faithfulness in their lives. By considering how God has guided and provided for them in the past, they can gain valuable insights and strengthen their desire to seek Him. This reflection helps them to recognize the importance of staying committed to their spiritual journey and finding new ways to grow in their faith. Psalm 119:105 says, "Thy word is a lamp unto my feet, and a light unto my path." This verse highlights the importance of regularly engaging with Scripture to illuminate one's path and maintain a strong desire for God.

Both hunters and Christians must also be mindful of distractions and obstacles that can diminish their desire. Hunters need to stay focused and avoid distractions that can lead them away from their goals or cause them to lose sight of their prey. This might involve tuning out negative voices, staying focused on their objectives, and maintaining a positive mindset. Similarly, Christians must be vigilant about the influences they allow into their lives, recognizing that distractions and negative influences can lead them away from their pursuit of God.

This vigilance involves testing the spirits, as 1 John 4:1 instructs, and being discerning about the sources of their spiritual nourishment. By maintaining a focus on God's truth and avoiding distractions, both hunters and Christians can stay committed to their goals and grow in their desire.

In conclusion, desire is a fundamental aspect of success and fulfillment in both hunting and the Christian life. For hunters, a strong desire to succeed drives their dedication, perseverance, and commitment to improving their skills and strategies. It fuels their passion for the hunt and motivates them to overcome challenges and achieve their goals. For Christians, desire is essential for seeking and growing closer to God. It drives their commitment to spiritual practices, their perseverance through trials, and their dedication to living according to God's will. Psalm 37:4 encapsulates this call to desire: "Delight thyself also in the LORD; and he shall give thee the desires of thine heart." By embracing the principles of nurturing desire in their respective pursuits, both hunters and Christians can achieve their goals, grow in their skills and faith, and live lives that honor God. Desire is a journey marked by continuous effort, learning, and a commitment to passion and dedication, leading to success and fulfillment in both hunting and the Christian life.

Chapter 17 Devotion

Devotion is a vital element in both hunting and the Christian life, embodying dedication, perseverance, and a wholehearted commitment to the task at hand. In hunting, successful hunters must exhibit unwavering devotion to their pursuit. This devotion is reflected in the time, effort, and resources they invest in preparing for the hunt. Hunters must be devoted to learning about their prey, understanding their habits, and mastering the skills needed to track and capture them. This involves studying animal behavior, practicing marksmanship, and honing their tracking abilities. Devotion to hunting also means being willing to endure the physical and mental challenges that come with it, such as waking up early, braving harsh weather, and spending long hours in the wilderness. Hunters who are devoted to their craft are more likely to succeed because they are willing to put in the necessary work and persist through difficulties. They approach each hunt with a sense of purpose and dedication, understanding that success is not guaranteed but is achieved through consistent effort and perseverance. This devotion is not just about the act of hunting itself but also about respecting nature and the ethical practices that ensure the sustainability of wildlife. Devoted hunters are mindful of conservation laws and ethical guidelines, ensuring that their actions contribute to the preservation of ecosystems and the responsible use of natural resources.

Similarly, in the Christian life, believers are called to be devoted to God, dedicating their lives to His service and seeking to honor Him in all they do. Devotion to God means presenting oneself as a living sacrifice, as stated in Romans 12:1: "I beseech you therefore, brethren, by the mercies of God, that ye present your bodies a living sacrifice, holy, acceptable unto God, which is your reasonable service." This verse emphasizes the idea of wholehearted commitment and dedication to God, urging believers to live in a way that is holy and pleasing to Him. Devotion to God involves regular prayer, studying the Bible, and participating in worship and fellowship. It means prioritizing one's relationship with God above all else and seeking to align one's life with His will. Just as hunters devote themselves to the pursuit of their prey, Christians devote themselves to the pursuit of a deeper relationship with God. This devotion drives them to grow in their faith, serve others, and live out the teachings of Christ. It helps them to persevere through trials, remain steadfast in their beliefs, and seek God's guidance in all aspects of life.

For both hunters and Christians, devotion involves a deep commitment and dedication to their pursuits. Hunters commit to the rigorous demands of hunting, often planning trips months in advance, investing in quality gear, and practicing their skills regularly. This commitment is driven by a passion for the hunt and a desire to succeed. Similarly, Christians commit to their spiritual journey, dedicating time and energy to grow in their faith and live according to God's will. This commitment involves regular participation in church activities, personal Bible study, and serving others. By nurturing their devotion to God, Christians find the strength and motivation to overcome obstacles and stay faithful in their walk with Him.

Devotion also requires perseverance and resilience. Hunters face numerous challenges, such as harsh weather, difficult terrain, and elusive prey. Their devotion helps them to persevere through these challenges, learning from each experience and continually striving to improve. Similarly, Christians face spiritual challenges, including temptations, doubts, and trials. Their devotion to God helps them to persevere, trusting in His promises and relying on His strength. James 1:12 says, "Blessed is the man that endureth temptation: for when he is tried, he shall receive the crown of life, which the Lord hath promised to them that love him." This verse encourages believers to remain steadfast in their faith, knowing that their devotion to God will be rewarded.

Both hunters and Christians benefit from the support and encouragement of their communities in nurturing their devotion. Hunters often share their passion with fellow hunters, forming bonds and learning from each other's experiences. This sense of community enhances their devotion, providing motivation and support. Similarly, Christians are part of a faith community that offers encouragement, accountability, and fellowship. Fellow believers can share insights, provide spiritual support, and pray for one another, helping to strengthen their collective devotion to God. Hebrews 10:24-25 highlights the importance of this community support: "And let us consider one another to provoke unto love and to good works: Not forsaking the assembling of ourselves together, as the manner of some is; but exhorting one another: and so much the more, as ye see the day approaching." This sense of community helps believers to stay focused on their spiritual goals and grow in their devotion to God.

Preparation is another key aspect of devotion. Hunters prepare by studying their prey, practicing their skills, and planning their hunts. This preparation is driven by a desire to be successful and to respect the art of hunting. Similarly, Christians prepare by immersing themselves in God's Word, spending time in prayer, and seeking to understand God's will. This spiritual preparation is motivated by a desire to know God more intimately and to live according to His purposes. By being intentional about their preparation, both hunters and Christians can ensure they are well-equipped to pursue their goals and overcome challenges.

Devotion also involves setting goals and striving for excellence. Hunters set goals for their hunts, such as tracking a specific animal or mastering a particular skill. These goals provide direction and motivation, helping them to stay focused and work diligently toward their objectives. Similarly, Christians set spiritual goals, such as deepening their prayer life, growing in their understanding of Scripture, or serving in their community. These goals help believers to stay focused on their spiritual journey and continually seek to grow in their faith. Philippians 3:14 says, "I press toward the mark for the prize of the high calling of God in Christ Jesus." This verse highlights the importance of setting spiritual goals and striving for excellence in one's faith.

Adaptability is another important aspect of devotion. Hunters must be adaptable, ready to adjust their plans based on changing conditions, such as weather, terrain, or animal behavior. This flexibility allows them to stay focused on their goals and respond effectively to challenges. Similarly, Christians must be adaptable in their spiritual journey, remaining open to God's leading and willing to change course when necessary. Life is full of unexpected twists and turns, and a rigid approach can lead to frustration and missed opportunities. By staying flexible and trusting in God's guidance, Christians can navigate these changes with confidence and faith.

Reflection and learning from experiences are also crucial for nurturing devotion. Hunters reflect on their successes and failures, learning from each experience to improve their skills and strategies. This reflective practice helps them to grow in their passion for hunting and their devotion to succeeding. Similarly, Christians grow in their faith by reflecting on their spiritual journey and recognizing God's faithfulness in their lives. By considering how God has guided and provided for them in the past, they can gain valuable insights and strengthen their devotion to Him. This reflection helps them to recognize the importance of staying committed to their spiritual journey and finding new ways to grow in their faith. Psalm 119:105 says, "Thy word is a lamp unto my feet, and a light unto my path." This verse highlights the importance of regularly engaging with Scripture to illuminate one's path and maintain strong devotion to God.

Both hunters and Christians must also be mindful of distractions and obstacles that can diminish their devotion. Hunters need to stay focused and avoid distractions that can lead them away from their goals or cause them to lose sight of their prey. This might involve tuning out negative voices, staying focused on their objectives, and maintaining a positive mindset. Similarly, Christians must be vigilant about the influences they allow into their lives, recognizing that distractions and negative influences can lead them away from their pursuit of God. This vigilance involves testing the spirits, as 1 John 4:1 instructs, and being discerning about the sources of their spiritual nourishment. By maintaining a focus on God's truth and avoiding distractions, both hunters and Christians can stay committed to their goals and grow in their devotion.

In conclusion, devotion is a fundamental aspect of success and fulfillment in both hunting and the Christian life. For hunters, devotion to the task drives their dedication, perseverance, and commitment to improving their skills and strategies. It fuels their passion for the hunt and motivates them to overcome challenges and achieve their goals. For Christians, devotion to God is essential for seeking and growing closer to Him. It drives their commitment to spiritual practices, their perseverance through trials, and their dedication to living according to God's will. Romans 12:1 encapsulates this call to devotion: "I beseech you therefore, brethren, by the mercies of God, that ye present your bodies a living sacrifice, holy, acceptable unto God, which is your reasonable service." By embracing the principles of nurturing devotion in their respective pursuits, both hunters and Christians can achieve their goals, grow in their skills and faith, and live lives that honor God. Devotion is a journey marked by continuous effort, learning, and a commitment to dedication and perseverance, leading to success and fulfillment in both hunting and the Christian life.

Chapter 18 Deliberation

Deliberation is a key aspect of both hunting and the Christian life, requiring careful thought, patience, and a commitment to making wise decisions. In hunting, deliberation is crucial before taking a shot. Hunters must assess numerous factors such as the distance to the target, the animal's behavior, the surrounding environment, and the potential risks involved. This careful consideration ensures that the shot is ethical, effective, and safe. Deliberation in hunting involves being patient and waiting for the right moment to take the shot. Rushing can lead to mistakes, such as missing the target or causing unnecessary suffering to the animal. Hunters learn to control their adrenaline and excitement, focusing on their breathing, aiming steadily, and making sure they have a clear and ethical shot. This process of deliberation requires experience, discipline, and a deep respect for the animal and the environment. Hunters who take the time to deliberate are more likely to succeed and to hunt responsibly, ensuring that their actions contribute to conservation efforts and the ethical treatment of wildlife. This thoughtful approach to hunting also involves planning and preparation, such as scouting locations, understanding animal habits, and practicing marksmanship regularly. By being deliberate in their actions, hunters can enhance their skills, increase their success rates, and ensure that they are respecting the natural world.

Similarly, in the Christian life, deliberation is essential for making decisions that align with God's will and reflect His teachings. Christians are called to meditate on God's Word and deliberate on His precepts before acting. Psalm 119:15 emphasizes this: "I will meditate in thy precepts, and have respect unto thy ways." This verse highlights the importance of taking time to reflect on Scripture and seeking God's guidance in all aspects of life. Deliberation in the Christian context involves studying the Bible, praying for wisdom, and seeking counsel from trusted spiritual mentors. By taking the time to meditate on God's

Word, Christians can gain a deeper understanding of His teachings and how to apply them in their daily lives. This process helps believers to make decisions that honor God, avoid sinful behavior, and grow in their faith. Deliberation also involves being patient and waiting on God's timing. Just as hunters wait for the right moment to take a shot, Christians must wait for God's guidance and trust that His timing is perfect. This patience is a sign of faith and trust in God's plan, allowing believers to act with confidence and purpose.

For both hunters and Christians, deliberation requires a combination of knowledge, patience, and a willingness to seek guidance. Hunters gain knowledge through experience, studying animal behavior, and practicing their skills. This knowledge helps them to make informed decisions and to deliberate effectively before taking a shot. Similarly, Christians gain knowledge by studying the Bible, engaging in prayer, and participating in church activities. This spiritual knowledge equips them to deliberate on God's Word and to make decisions that reflect His will. Patience is also crucial in the process of deliberation. Hunters must be patient and wait for the right moment, knowing that haste can lead to mistakes and missed opportunities. Similarly, Christians must be patient in their spiritual journey, trusting that God will reveal His will in His perfect timing. This patience allows believers to act thoughtfully and to avoid impulsive decisions that may lead them away from God's path.

Both hunters and Christians benefit from the guidance and support of their communities in the process of deliberation. Hunters often consult with more experienced hunters, seeking advice and learning from their expertise. This sense of community and shared knowledge enhances their ability to deliberate and make wise decisions. Similarly, Christians are part of a faith community that offers support, encouragement, and accountability. Fellow believers can provide insights, share their own experiences, and pray for one another, helping to strengthen their collective ability to deliberate on God's

Word. Hebrews 10:24-25 highlights the importance of this community support: "And let us consider one another to provoke unto love and to good works: Not forsaking the assembling of ourselves together, as the manner of some is; but exhorting one another: and so much the more, as ye see the day approaching." This sense of community helps believers to stay focused on their spiritual goals and to grow in their ability to deliberate thoughtfully.

Preparation is another key aspect of effective deliberation. Hunters prepare by studying their prey, practicing their skills, and planning their hunts. This preparation allows them to deliberate effectively in the field, ensuring that they can make quick and accurate decisions when the moment arises. Similarly, Christians prepare by immersing themselves in God's Word, spending time in prayer, and seeking to understand God's will. This spiritual preparation equips them to deliberate on God's Word and to act in a way that honors Him. By being intentional about their preparation, both hunters and Christians can ensure they are well-equipped to pursue their goals and to make wise decisions.

Reflection and learning from experiences are also crucial for effective deliberation. Hunters reflect on their successes and failures, learning from each experience to improve their skills and decision-making. This reflective practice helps them to grow in their ability to deliberate and to hunt responsibly. Similarly, Christians grow in their faith by reflecting on their spiritual journey and recognizing God's faithfulness in their lives. By considering how God has guided and provided for them in the past, they can gain valuable insights and strengthen their ability to deliberate on His Word. This reflection helps them to recognize the importance of staying committed to their spiritual journey and finding new ways to grow in their faith. Psalm 119:105 says, "Thy word is a lamp unto my feet, and a light unto my path." This verse highlights the importance of regularly engaging with

Scripture to illuminate one's path and to maintain strong deliberation on God's Word.

Both hunters and Christians must also be mindful of distractions and obstacles that can hinder their ability to deliberate effectively. Hunters need to stay focused and avoid distractions that can cause them to lose sight of their target or make hasty decisions. This might involve tuning out negative voices, staying focused on their objectives, and maintaining a positive mindset. Similarly, Christians must be vigilant about the influences they allow into their lives, recognizing that distractions and negative influences can lead them away from their pursuit of God. This vigilance involves testing the spirits, as 1 John 4:1 instructs, and being discerning about the sources of their spiritual nourishment. By maintaining a focus on God's truth and avoiding distractions, both hunters and Christians can stay committed to their goals and grow in their ability to deliberate effectively.

Adaptability is another important aspect of deliberation. Hunters must be adaptable, ready to adjust their plans based on changing conditions, such as weather, terrain, or animal behavior. This flexibility allows them to stay focused on their goals and to respond effectively to challenges. Similarly, Christians must be adaptable in their spiritual journey, remaining open to God's leading and willing to change course when necessary. Life is full of unexpected twists and turns, and a rigid approach can lead to frustration and missed opportunities. By staying flexible and trusting in God's guidance, Christians can navigate these changes with confidence and faith.

In conclusion, deliberation is a fundamental aspect of success and fulfillment in both hunting and the Christian life. For hunters, deliberation before taking a shot ensures that their actions are ethical, effective, and safe. It involves a combination of knowledge, patience, and experience, as well as the support of a knowledgeable community. For Christians, deliberation on God's Word is essential for making decisions that align with His will and reflect His teachings. It involves regular study of Scripture, prayer, and fellowship with other believers, as well as a deep reliance on the Holy Spirit. Psalm 119:15 encapsulates this call to deliberation: "I will meditate in thy precepts, and have respect unto thy ways." By embracing the principles of effective deliberation in their respective pursuits, both hunters and Christians can achieve their goals, grow in their skills and faith, and live lives that honor God. Deliberation is a journey marked by continuous effort, learning, and a commitment to thoughtful and wise decision-making, leading to success and fulfillment in both hunting and the Christian life.

Chapter 19 Discovery

Discovery is an exciting and essential part of both hunting and the Christian life, bringing new insights, experiences, and growth. For hunters, the thrill of discovering new areas and trails is a significant aspect of their pursuit. Each hunting expedition can lead to the discovery of uncharted territories, hidden paths, and secret spots where wildlife thrives. This sense of exploration drives hunters to venture further into the wilderness, seeking out new places to set up blinds, track animals, and immerse themselves in nature. Discovering new areas often requires careful observation, knowledge of the terrain, and an adventurous spirit. Hunters must be attuned to their surroundings, looking for signs of animal activity such as tracks, scat, and feeding areas. They may also use maps, GPS devices, and tips from other hunters to uncover promising locations. This process of discovery enhances their hunting skills, broadens their understanding of wildlife behavior, and deepens their connection to the natural world. The excitement of finding a new trail or a perfect hunting spot is rewarding and fuels their passion for the hunt, encouraging them to continue exploring and learning.

Similarly, in the Christian life, discovery is a vital aspect of spiritual growth and deepening one's relationship with God. Christians are called to discover new truths in God's Word, seeking wisdom and understanding through diligent study and reflection. Proverbs 2:4-5 emphasizes this pursuit: "If thou seekest her as silver, and searchest for her as for hid treasures; Then shalt thou understand the fear of the LORD, and find the knowledge of God." This verse highlights the importance of actively seeking God's wisdom and valuing it as one would a hidden treasure. The process of discovering new truths in Scripture involves regular Bible study, meditation, and prayer. As Christians delve into God's Word, they uncover deeper meanings, fresh insights, and applications for their lives. Each discovery in the Bible brings them closer to God, revealing His character, promises, and guidance. This spiritual exploration fosters a deeper understanding of their faith and helps them to grow in wisdom and godliness.

For both hunters and Christians, discovery requires a sense of curiosity, a willingness to explore, and a dedication to learning. Hunters often approach each outing with an eagerness to discover something new, whether it's a prime hunting location, an animal's habits, or a unique natural feature. This curiosity keeps their passion for hunting alive and drives them to continually seek out new experiences and knowledge. Similarly, Christians are encouraged to approach their spiritual journey with a hunger for discovery, eagerly exploring the depths of God's Word and seeking His truth. This desire for discovery helps them to grow in their faith, understand God's will, and live according to His purposes.

Both hunters and Christians benefit from the guidance and support of their communities in the process of discovery. Hunters often share their findings with fellow hunters, exchanging tips and knowledge about new areas and trails. This sense of community and shared exploration enhances their ability to discover and learn. Similarly, Christians are part of a faith community that offers support, encouragement, and shared insights. Fellow believers can provide wisdom, share their own discoveries in Scripture, and pray for one another, helping to strengthen their collective understanding of God's Word. Hebrews 10:24-25 emphasizes the importance of this community support: "And let us consider one another to provoke unto love and to good works: Not forsaking the assembling of ourselves together, as the manner of some is; but exhorting one another: and so much the more, as ye see the day approaching." This sense of community helps believers to stay focused on their spiritual goals and to grow in their ability to discover new truths.

Preparation is another key aspect of effective discovery. Hunters prepare by studying maps, understanding animal behavior, and equipping themselves with the necessary tools for exploration. This preparation allows them to navigate effectively and make the most of their discoveries in the field. Similarly, Christians prepare for spiritual discovery by immersing themselves in God's Word, spending time in prayer, and seeking to understand God's will. This spiritual preparation equips them to uncover new truths and to apply these insights to their lives. By being intentional about their preparation, both hunters and Christians can ensure they are well-equipped to pursue their goals and to make meaningful discoveries.

Reflection and learning from experiences are also crucial for effective discovery. Hunters reflect on their outings, analyzing what worked and what didn't, and applying these lessons to future expeditions. This reflective practice helps them to grow in their ability to discover new areas and to enhance their hunting skills. Similarly, Christians grow in their faith by reflecting on their spiritual journey and recognizing God's faithfulness in their lives. By considering how God has guided and provided for them in the past, they can gain valuable insights and strengthen their ability to discover new truths in Scripture. This reflection helps them to recognize the importance of staying committed to their spiritual journey and finding new ways to grow in their faith. Psalm 119:105 says, "Thy word is a lamp unto my feet, and a light unto my path." This verse highlights the importance of regularly engaging with Scripture to illuminate one's path and to maintain a strong commitment to discovery.

Both hunters and Christians must also be mindful of distractions and obstacles that can hinder their ability to discover effectively. Hunters need to stay focused and avoid distractions that can cause them to miss signs of animal activity or to overlook promising trails. This might involve tuning out negative voices, staying focused on their objectives, and maintaining a positive mindset. Similarly, Christians must be vigilant about the influences they allow into their lives, recognizing that distractions and negative influences can lead them away from their pursuit of God. This vigilance involves testing the spirits, as 1 John 4:1 instructs, and being discerning about the sources of their spiritual nourishment. By maintaining a focus on God's truth and avoiding distractions, both hunters and Christians can stay committed to their goals and grow in their ability to discover effectively.

Adaptability is another important aspect of discovery. Hunters must be adaptable, ready to adjust their plans based on changing conditions, such as weather, terrain, or animal behavior. This flexibility allows them to stay focused on their goals and to respond effectively to challenges. Similarly, Christians must be adaptable in their spiritual journey, remaining open to God's leading and willing to change course when necessary. Life is full of unexpected twists and turns, and a rigid approach can lead to frustration and missed opportunities. By staying flexible and trusting in God's guidance, Christians can navigate these changes with confidence and faith.

In conclusion, discovery is a fundamental aspect of success and fulfillment in both hunting and the Christian life. For hunters, discovering new areas and trails enhances their skills, broadens their understanding of wildlife, and deepens their connection to the natural world. It involves a combination of curiosity, knowledge, and experience, as well as the support of a knowledgeable community. For Christians, discovering new truths in God's Word is essential for spiritual growth and deepening one's relationship with God. It involves regular study of Scripture, prayer, and fellowship with other believers, as well as a deep reliance on the Holy Spirit. Proverbs 2:4-5 encapsulates this call to discovery: "If thou seekest her as silver, and searchest for her as for hid treasures; Then shalt thou understand the fear of the LORD, and find the knowledge of God." By embracing the principles of effective discovery in their respective pursuits, both hunters and Christians can achieve their goals, grow in their skills and faith, and live lives that honor God. Discovery is a journey marked by continuous effort, learning, and a commitment to exploration and growth, leading to success and fulfillment in both hunting and the Christian life.

Chapter 20 Direction

Direction is a crucial aspect of both hunting and the Christian life, involving careful guidance, a clear sense of purpose, and the ability to navigate challenges successfully. In hunting, having a clear sense of direction is essential for ensuring a successful and safe hunt. Hunters must know where they are going, understand the terrain, and be aware of the best routes to take to find their prey. This involves studying maps, using compasses or GPS devices, and paying close attention to landmarks and natural signs. Hunters need to plan their path carefully, considering factors such as wind direction, animal trails, and potential hazards in the environment. A clear sense of direction helps hunters stay focused on their goals and avoid getting lost or encountering dangerous situations. It requires experience, knowledge, and the ability to adapt to changing conditions. Hunters who are skilled in navigation can effectively track their prey, position themselves advantageously, and make strategic decisions that increase their chances of success. This sense of direction also fosters confidence, as hunters can move through the wilderness with a sense of purpose and clarity, knowing that they are on the right path.

Similarly, in the Christian life, having spiritual direction is essential for living a life that aligns with God's will and purpose. Christians seek spiritual direction through prayer, reading the Bible, and listening to the guidance of the Holy Spirit. Isaiah 30:21 highlights the importance of divine guidance: "And thine ears shall hear a word behind thee, saying, This is the way, walk ye in it." This verse emphasizes the idea that God provides direction to His followers, guiding them along the right path. Christians believe that God has a plan for each person, and seeking His direction helps them to navigate the complexities of life with wisdom and faith. Spiritual direction involves discerning God's voice, understanding His teachings, and applying them to everyday decisions. By seeking God's direction, Christians can find clarity and purpose, making choices that reflect His will and lead to a fulfilling life. This process requires a deep relationship with God, regular engagement with Scripture, and a willingness to listen and obey His guidance.

For both hunters and Christians, direction involves a combination of preparation, knowledge, and adaptability. Hunters prepare by studying their environment, practicing their navigation skills, and equipping themselves with the necessary tools for the journey. This preparation helps them to navigate effectively and make informed decisions in the field. Similarly, Christians prepare by immersing themselves in God's Word, spending time in prayer, and seeking fellowship with other believers. This spiritual preparation equips them to discern God's direction and respond to His leading. By grounding themselves in their faith and remaining attentive to God's guidance, Christians can navigate life's challenges with confidence and assurance.

Adaptability is another crucial aspect of maintaining the right direction. Hunters must be able to adapt to changing conditions, such as shifting wind patterns, unexpected weather, or the sudden movement of their prey. This flexibility allows them to stay on course and adjust their strategies as needed. Similarly, Christians must be adaptable in their spiritual journey, remaining open to God's leading and willing to change course when necessary. Life is full of unexpected twists and turns, and a rigid approach can lead to frustration and missed opportunities. By staying flexible and trusting in God's sovereignty, Christians can navigate these changes with confidence and faith.

Patience and perseverance are also essential components of maintaining the right direction. Hunters often need to wait for long periods, remaining still and patient, to avoid alerting their prey and to seize the right moment for action. This patience is a testament to their dedication and discipline, ensuring they do not rush and risk losing their opportunity. Similarly, Christians are called to be patient and persevere in their faith, trusting that God will provide the wisdom and guidance they need. James 1:5 encourages believers to seek God's wisdom: "If any of you lack wisdom, let him ask of God, that giveth to all men liberally, and upbraideth not; and it shall be given him." This verse reminds Christians that God is the source of all wisdom and that they can rely on Him for direction in every situation.

Both hunters and Christians benefit from the support and guidance of their communities in maintaining the right direction. Hunters often learn from more experienced hunters, gaining insights and tips that help them make better decisions in the field. This sense of community and shared knowledge enhances their ability to navigate effectively and succeed. Similarly, Christians are part of a faith community that provides support, encouragement, and accountability. Fellow believers can offer wisdom, share their experiences, and pray for one another, helping to strengthen their resolve and keep them on the right path. Hebrews 10:24-25 highlights the importance of this community support: "And let us consider one another to provoke unto love and to good works: Not forsaking the assembling of ourselves together, as the manner of some is; but exhorting one another: and so much the more, as ye see the day approaching." This sense of community helps believers stay grounded in their faith and grow in their ability to discern God's direction.

Reflection and learning from experiences are crucial for maintaining the right direction. Hunters reflect on their experiences, analyzing what worked and what didn't, and applying these lessons to future hunts. This reflective practice helps them improve their skills and decision-making, ensuring they are better equipped for future challenges. Similarly, Christians grow in their ability to discern God's direction through reflection and learning. By looking back on their spiritual journey and considering how God has guided them, they can gain valuable insights and strengthen their faith. This reflection helps them recognize areas where they need to be more attentive to God's leading and committed to living according to His will. Psalm 119:105 says, "Thy word is a lamp unto my feet, and a light unto my path." This verse highlights the importance of regularly engaging with Scripture to illuminate one's path and maintain the right spiritual direction.

Both hunters and Christians must also be aware of the potential for distractions and obstacles that can lead them off course. Hunters need to stay focused and avoid distractions that can cause them to lose sight of their target or miss important signs in the environment. This might involve tuning out negative voices or staying focused on their goals despite challenging conditions. Similarly, Christians must be vigilant about the influences they allow into their lives, recognizing that distractions and negative influences can lead them away from God's path. This vigilance involves testing the spirits, as 1 John 4:1 instructs, and being discerning about the sources of their spiritual nourishment. By maintaining a focus on God's truth and avoiding distractions, both hunters and Christians can stay on course and achieve their goals.

In conclusion, direction is a fundamental aspect of success and fulfillment in both hunting and the Christian life. For hunters, maintaining the right direction involves careful planning, preparation, and adaptability, ensuring they can navigate the challenges of the natural environment and position themselves for success. It requires patience, perseverance, and the support of a knowledgeable community. For Christians, direction means seeking God's guidance and aligning their lives with His will. It involves regular study of Scripture, prayer, and fellowship with other believers, as well as a deep reliance on the Holy Spirit. Isaiah 30:21 encapsulates this call to divine guidance: "And thine ears shall hear a word behind thee, saying, This is the way, walk ye in it." By embracing the principles of maintaining the right direction in their respective pursuits, both hunters and Christians can achieve their goals, grow in their skills and faith, and live lives that honor God. Direction is a journey marked by continuous effort, learning, and a commitment to following the right path, leading to success and fulfillment in both hunting and the Christian life.

Chapter 21 Discretion

Discretion is a vital quality in both hunting and the Christian life, serving as a guide to making wise decisions, avoiding danger, and acting with prudence. For hunters, discretion is essential for staying safe and ensuring a successful hunt. Hunters must use their judgment to assess risks and make careful decisions about when to move, when to stay still, and when to take a shot. This involves being aware of their surroundings, understanding animal behavior, and anticipating potential hazards. For example, a hunter must decide whether a particular path is safe to take or if it might lead to a dangerous encounter with wildlife or difficult terrain. They must also be cautious about making noise, leaving scents, or taking actions that could alert their prey or attract predators. Discretion helps hunters avoid accidents and maintain the element of surprise, which is crucial for a successful hunt. It requires patience, experience, and a keen awareness of the environment. Hunters who exercise discretion are more likely to stay safe, respect the natural world, and achieve their goals.

Similarly, in the Christian life, discretion is important for living wisely and avoiding spiritual pitfalls. Christians are called to use discretion in their actions, ensuring that their behavior aligns with God's teachings and reflects His love and wisdom. Proverbs 2:11 emphasizes the protective power of discretion: "Discretion shall preserve thee, understanding shall keep thee." This verse highlights the role of discretion in guiding believers to make decisions that honor God and protect their spiritual well-being. Discretion in the Christian context involves careful consideration of one's words, actions, and choices. It means avoiding situations that could lead to temptation or compromise one's values. For instance, a Christian might use discretion by choosing not to engage in gossip, avoiding harmful relationships, or steering clear of environments that could lead to sinful behavior. Discretion also involves seeking God's guidance through prayer and

Scripture, allowing His wisdom to direct one's path. By exercising discretion, Christians can navigate life's challenges with integrity and faithfulness, reflecting God's character in their actions.

For both hunters and Christians, discretion involves a combination of knowledge, experience, and a willingness to seek guidance. Hunters gain knowledge through experience, learning from each outing and refining their skills over time. This knowledge helps them to make informed decisions and to use discretion effectively in the field. Similarly, Christians gain knowledge by studying the Bible, engaging in prayer, and seeking counsel from wise and trusted individuals. This spiritual knowledge equips them to exercise discretion in their daily lives and to make choices that honor God. Experience also plays a crucial role in developing discretion. Hunters learn from their successes and failures, becoming more adept at recognizing potential dangers and making wise decisions. Similarly, Christians grow in their ability to use discretion through their experiences, learning from their mistakes and seeking to align their lives more closely with God's will.

Both hunters and Christians benefit from the support and encouragement of their communities in exercising discretion. Hunters often share their experiences with fellow hunters, learning from each other's insights and advice. This sense of community and shared knowledge enhances their ability to use discretion and to make wise decisions in the field. Similarly, Christians are part of a faith community that offers support, accountability, and encouragement. Fellow believers can provide wisdom, share their own experiences, and pray for one another, helping to strengthen their collective ability to exercise discretion. Hebrews 10:24-25 highlights the importance of this community support: "And let us consider one another to provoke unto love and to good works: Not forsaking the assembling of ourselves together, as the manner of some is; but exhorting one another: and so much the more, as ye see the day approaching." This sense of community helps believers to stay focused on their spiritual goals and to grow in their ability to exercise discretion.

Preparation is another key aspect of effective discretion. Hunters prepare by studying their prey, practicing their skills, and planning their hunts. This preparation allows them to use discretion effectively in the field, ensuring that they can make quick and accurate decisions when the moment arises. Similarly, Christians prepare for exercising discretion by immersing themselves in God's Word, spending time in prayer, and seeking to understand God's will. This spiritual preparation equips them to discern God's direction and to act in a way that honors Him. By being intentional about their preparation, both hunters and Christians can ensure they are well-equipped to pursue their goals and to make wise decisions.

Reflection and learning from experiences are also crucial for effective discretion. Hunters reflect on their outings, analyzing what worked and what didn't, and applying these lessons to future expeditions. This reflective practice helps them to grow in their ability to use discretion and to enhance their hunting skills. Similarly, Christians grow in their faith by reflecting on their spiritual journey and recognizing God's faithfulness in their lives. By considering how God has guided and provided for them in the past, they can gain valuable insights and strengthen their ability to exercise discretion. This reflection helps them to recognize the importance of staying committed to their spiritual journey and finding new ways to grow in their faith. Psalm 119:105 says, "Thy word is a lamp unto my feet, and a light unto my path." This verse highlights the importance of regularly engaging with Scripture to illuminate one's path and to maintain strong discretion. Both hunters and Christians must also be mindful of distractions and obstacles that can hinder their ability to exercise discretion effectively. Hunters need to stay focused and avoid distractions that can cause them to lose sight of their target or make hasty decisions. This might involve tuning out negative voices, staying focused on their objectives, and maintaining a positive mindset. Similarly, Christians must be vigilant about the influences they allow into their lives, recognizing that distractions and negative influences can lead them away from their pursuit of God. This vigilance involves testing the spirits, as 1 John 4:1 instructs, and being discerning about the sources of their spiritual nourishment. By maintaining a focus on God's truth and avoiding distractions, both hunters and Christians can stay committed to their goals and grow in their ability to exercise discretion.

Adaptability is another important aspect of discretion. Hunters must be adaptable, ready to adjust their plans based on changing conditions, such as weather, terrain, or animal behavior. This flexibility allows them to stay focused on their goals and to respond effectively to challenges. Similarly, Christians must be adaptable in their spiritual journey, remaining open to God's leading and willing to change course when necessary. Life is full of unexpected twists and turns, and a rigid approach can lead to frustration and missed opportunities. By staying flexible and trusting in God's guidance, Christians can navigate these changes with confidence and faith.

In conclusion, discretion is a fundamental aspect of success and fulfillment in both hunting and the Christian life. For hunters, using discretion helps them stay safe, make wise decisions, and achieve their goals. It involves a combination of knowledge, experience, and careful judgment, as well as the support of a knowledgeable community. For Christians, exercising discretion is essential for living a life that aligns with God's will and reflects His teachings. It involves regular study of Scripture, prayer, and fellowship with other believers, as well as a deep reliance on the Holy Spirit. Proverbs 2:11 encapsulates this call to discretion: "Discretion shall preserve thee, understanding shall keep thee." By embracing the principles of effective discretion in their respective pursuits, both hunters and Christians can achieve their goals, grow in their skills and faith, and live lives that honor God. Discretion is a journey marked by continuous effort, learning, and a commitment to thoughtful and wise decision-making, leading to success and fulfillment in both hunting and the Christian life.

Chapter 22 Drive

Drive is an essential quality in both hunting and the Christian life, providing the motivation and determination needed to pursue goals and overcome challenges. In hunting, a strong drive is crucial for staying committed and pushing forward despite difficulties. Hunters often face long hours, harsh weather conditions, and the physical demands of tracking and waiting for their prey. This requires a deep-seated drive to keep going, even when the circumstances are tough. Hunters must be passionate about their pursuit, dedicating time and effort to honing their skills, understanding animal behavior, and planning their expeditions. This drive helps them to remain focused, patient, and resilient, knowing that success is not guaranteed but earned through perseverance and hard work. The drive to succeed in hunting is fueled by a love for the outdoors, the thrill of the chase, and the satisfaction of a successful hunt. It pushes hunters to wake up early, endure discomfort, and continually improve their techniques. Without this drive, the challenges of hunting could easily lead to discouragement and giving up. Instead, a strong drive enables hunters to stay motivated, learn from their experiences, and ultimately achieve their goals.

Similarly, in the Christian life, spiritual drive is essential for pursuing God's will and living a life that honors Him. Christians are called to have a strong drive to grow in their faith, serve others, and follow God's guidance. Philippians 3:14 emphasizes this pursuit: "I press toward the mark for the prize of the high calling of God in Christ Jesus." This verse highlights the importance of striving toward spiritual goals with determination and focus. A strong spiritual drive helps Christians to remain committed to their faith, even when faced with trials, temptations, and setbacks. It motivates them to spend time in prayer, study the Bible, and engage in worship and fellowship with other believers. This drive also inspires Christians to serve their communities, share the gospel, and live out the teachings of Christ in their daily lives. By maintaining a strong spiritual drive, Christians can overcome obstacles, grow in their relationship with God, and make a positive impact on the world around them.

For both hunters and Christians, drive involves a combination of passion, perseverance, and a willingness to push through challenges. Hunters must be passionate about their pursuit, finding joy and fulfillment in the process of hunting. This passion fuels their drive, giving them the energy and determination to keep going, even when the hunt is difficult. Similarly, Christians must have a passion for their faith, finding joy in their relationship with God and the purpose He has given them. This passion drives them to pursue spiritual growth, serve others, and live according to God's will. Perseverance is also a key component of drive. Hunters often face setbacks, such as missed shots, bad weather, or elusive prey. A strong drive helps them to persevere through these challenges, learning from their experiences and continuing to pursue their goals. Similarly, Christians face trials and temptations that can test their faith. A strong spiritual drive helps them to persevere, trusting in God's promises and relying on His strength. James 1:12 says, "Blessed is the man that endureth temptation: for when he is tried, he shall receive the crown of life, which the Lord hath promised to them that love him." This verse encourages believers to remain steadfast in their faith, knowing that their drive to follow God will be rewarded.

Both hunters and Christians benefit from the support and encouragement of their communities in nurturing their drive. Hunters often share their passion with fellow hunters, forming bonds and learning from each other's experiences. This sense of community enhances their drive, providing motivation and support. Similarly, Christians are part of a faith community that offers encouragement, accountability, and fellowship. Fellow believers can provide wisdom, share their own experiences, and pray for one another, helping to strengthen their collective drive to pursue God's will. Hebrews 10:24-25 highlights the importance of this community support: "And let us consider one another to provoke unto love and to good works: Not forsaking the assembling of ourselves together, as the manner of some is; but exhorting one another: and so much the more, as ye see the day approaching." This sense of community helps believers to stay focused on their spiritual goals and grow in their drive to follow God.

Preparation is another key aspect of drive. Hunters prepare by studying their prey, practicing their skills, and planning their hunts. This preparation allows them to pursue their goals with confidence and determination, knowing they are well-equipped to handle the challenges they may face. Similarly, Christians prepare by immersing themselves in God's Word, spending time in prayer, and seeking to understand God's will. This spiritual preparation equips them to pursue their spiritual goals with drive and determination. By being intentional about their preparation, both hunters and Christians can ensure they are well-equipped to pursue their goals and to overcome challenges.

Reflection and learning from experiences are also crucial for nurturing drive. Hunters reflect on their successes and failures, learning from each experience to improve their skills and strategies. This reflective practice helps them to grow in their passion for hunting and their drive to succeed. Similarly, Christians grow in their faith by reflecting on their spiritual journey and recognizing God's faithfulness in their lives. By considering how God has guided and provided for them in the past, they can gain valuable insights and strengthen their drive to seek Him. This reflection helps them to recognize the importance of staying committed to their spiritual journey and finding new ways to grow in their faith. Psalm 119:105 says, "Thy word is a lamp unto my feet, and a light unto my path." This verse highlights the importance of regularly engaging with Scripture to illuminate one's path and maintain a strong drive to follow God.

Both hunters and Christians must also be mindful of distractions and obstacles that can diminish their drive. Hunters need to stay focused and avoid distractions that can lead them away from their goals or cause them to lose sight of their prey. This might involve tuning out negative voices, staying focused on their objectives, and maintaining a positive mindset. Similarly, Christians must be vigilant about the influences they allow into their lives, recognizing that distractions and negative influences can lead them away from their pursuit of God. This vigilance involves testing the spirits, as 1 John 4:1 instructs, and being discerning about the sources of their spiritual nourishment. By maintaining a focus on God's truth and avoiding distractions, both hunters and Christians can stay committed to their goals and grow in their drive.

Adaptability is another important aspect of drive. Hunters must be adaptable, ready to adjust their plans based on changing conditions, such as weather, terrain, or animal behavior. This flexibility allows them to stay focused on their goals and respond effectively to challenges. Similarly, Christians must be adaptable in their spiritual journey, remaining open to God's leading and willing to change course when necessary. Life is full of unexpected twists and turns, and a rigid approach can lead to frustration and missed opportunities. By staying flexible and trusting in God's guidance, Christians can navigate these changes with confidence and faith.

In conclusion, drive is a fundamental aspect of success and fulfillment in both hunting and the Christian life. For hunters, a strong drive to succeed drives their dedication, perseverance, and commitment to improving their skills and strategies. It fuels their passion for the hunt and motivates them to overcome challenges and achieve their goals. For Christians, spiritual drive is essential for seeking and growing closer to God. It drives their commitment to spiritual practices, their perseverance through trials, and their dedication to living according to God's will. Philippians 3:14 encapsulates this call to drive: "I press toward the mark for the prize of the high calling of God in Christ Jesus." By embracing the principles of nurturing drive in their respective pursuits, both hunters and Christians can achieve their goals, grow in their skills and faith, and live lives that honor God. Drive is a journey marked by continuous effort, learning, and a commitment to passion and perseverance, leading to success and fulfillment in both hunting and the Christian life.

Chapter 23 Diligence

Diligence is a critical trait in both hunting and the Christian life, requiring persistent effort, careful attention, and unwavering dedication. In hunting, diligence is essential for success. Hunters must be diligent in their preparation, which includes studying the habits and habitats of their prey, practicing their marksmanship, and ensuring they have the necessary equipment in good working order. This preparation is not a one-time effort but an ongoing process that requires regular practice and constant learning. Once in the field, hunters must remain diligent, paying close attention to their surroundings, tracking signs of wildlife, and being ready to seize opportunities when they arise. This means getting up early, sometimes before dawn, and spending long hours in often harsh and uncomfortable conditions. Hunters who are diligent do not easily give up; they remain focused and patient, knowing that success often comes to those who persist through challenges and setbacks. Diligence in hunting also involves ethical practices, such as following conservation laws, respecting wildlife, and ensuring that their actions do not harm the environment. This level of commitment ensures that hunting remains sustainable and respectful of nature.

Similarly, in the Christian life, diligence is essential for growing in faith and living according to God's will. Christians are called to be diligent in their spiritual practices, such as prayer, reading the Bible, and participating in church activities. This means setting aside regular time for these activities and making them a priority, even when life gets busy or distractions arise. Diligence in faith involves continually seeking to understand God's Word more deeply and applying it to one's life. Hebrews 6:11 underscores the importance of this persistence: "And we desire that every one of you do shew the same diligence to the full assurance of hope unto the end." This verse encourages believers to remain diligent in their faith journey, maintaining their hope and commitment until the end. Being diligent in the Christian life also means living out one's faith through actions, such as serving others, sharing the gospel, and striving to exhibit the fruits of the Spirit in daily interactions. Just as hunters must be patient and persistent, Christians are called to persevere through trials and temptations, trusting that their efforts will be rewarded by God's faithfulness.

For both hunters and Christians, diligence involves a combination of preparation, focus, and resilience. Hunters prepare by studying their prey, practicing their skills, and planning their hunts meticulously. This preparation allows them to approach each hunt with confidence and readiness, knowing they have done everything possible to ensure success. Similarly, Christians prepare for their spiritual journey by immersing themselves in God's Word, spending time in prayer, and seeking fellowship with other believers. This spiritual preparation equips them to face life's challenges with faith and strength, relying on God's guidance and support. Focus is also a crucial aspect of diligence. Hunters must remain focused on their goals, keeping their attention on their surroundings and the task at hand. Distractions can lead to missed opportunities or mistakes, so maintaining focus is essential for success. Similarly, Christians must stay focused on their relationship with God and their spiritual goals. This means avoiding distractions that can lead them away from their faith and staying committed to their spiritual practices.

Resilience is another key component of diligence. Hunters often face setbacks, such as missed shots, bad weather, or elusive prey. A diligent hunter does not give up in the face of these challenges but instead learns from each experience and continues to persevere. Similarly, Christians face trials and difficulties in their faith journey. Diligence in faith means trusting in God's promises and continuing to follow Him, even when the path is tough. James 1:12 speaks to this perseverance: "Blessed is the man that endureth temptation: for when he is tried, he shall receive the crown of life, which the Lord hath promised to them that love him." This verse encourages believers to remain steadfast, knowing that their diligent efforts will be rewarded.

Both hunters and Christians benefit from the support and encouragement of their communities in maintaining diligence. Hunters often share their experiences and knowledge with fellow hunters, learning from each other and providing mutual support. This sense of community enhances their ability to stay diligent and motivated. Similarly, Christians are part of a faith community that offers support, accountability, and encouragement. Fellow believers can provide wisdom, share their own experiences, and pray for one another, helping to strengthen their collective diligence in following God. Hebrews 10:24-25 highlights the importance of this community support: "And let us consider one another to provoke unto love and to good works: Not forsaking the assembling of ourselves together, as the manner of some is; but exhorting one another: and so much the more, as ye see the day approaching." This sense of community helps believers to stay focused on their spiritual goals and to grow in their diligence.

Preparation is another key aspect of effective diligence. Hunters prepare by studying their prey, practicing their skills, and planning their hunts. This preparation allows them to pursue their goals with confidence and determination, knowing they are well-equipped to handle the challenges they may face. Similarly, Christians prepare for exercising diligence by immersing themselves in God's Word, spending time in prayer, and seeking to understand God's will. This spiritual preparation equips them to pursue their spiritual goals with drive and determination. By being intentional about their preparation, both hunters and Christians can ensure they are well-equipped to pursue their goals and to overcome challenges.

Reflection and learning from experiences are also crucial for effective diligence. Hunters reflect on their outings, analyzing what worked and what didn't, and applying these lessons to future expeditions. This reflective practice helps them to grow in their ability to use diligence and to enhance their hunting skills. Similarly, Christians grow in their faith by reflecting on their spiritual journey and recognizing God's faithfulness in their lives. By considering how God has guided and provided for them in the past, they can gain valuable insights and strengthen their ability to exercise diligence. This reflection helps them to recognize the importance of staying committed to their spiritual journey and finding new ways to grow in their faith. Psalm 119:105 says, "Thy word is a lamp unto my feet, and a light unto my path." This verse highlights the importance of regularly engaging with Scripture to illuminate one's path and to maintain strong discretion.

Both hunters and Christians must also be mindful of distractions and obstacles that can hinder their ability to exercise discretion effectively. Hunters need to stay focused and avoid distractions that can cause them to lose sight of their target or make hasty decisions. This might involve tuning out negative voices, staying focused on their objectives, and maintaining a positive mindset. Similarly, Christians must be vigilant about the influences they allow into their lives, recognizing that distractions and negative influences can lead them away from their pursuit of God. This vigilance involves testing the spirits, as 1 John 4:1 instructs, and being discerning about the sources of their spiritual nourishment. By maintaining a focus on God's truth and avoiding distractions, both hunters and Christians can stay committed to their goals and grow in their ability to exercise discretion.

Adaptability is another important aspect of discretion. Hunters must be adaptable, ready to adjust their plans based on changing conditions, such as weather, terrain, or animal behavior. This flexibility allows them to stay focused on their goals and to respond effectively to challenges. Similarly, Christians must be adaptable in their spiritual journey, remaining open to God's leading and willing to change course when necessary. Life is full of unexpected twists and turns, and a rigid approach can lead to frustration and missed opportunities. By staying flexible and trusting in God's guidance, Christians can navigate these changes with confidence and faith.

In conclusion, diligence is a fundamental aspect of success and fulfillment in both hunting and the Christian life. For hunters, being diligent helps them stay safe, make wise decisions, and achieve their goals. It involves a combination of knowledge, experience, and careful judgment, as well as the support of a knowledgeable community. For Christians, exercising diligence is essential for living a life that aligns with God's will and reflects His teachings. It involves regular study of Scripture, prayer, and fellowship with other believers, as well as a deep reliance on the Holy Spirit. Hebrews 6:11 encapsulates this call to diligence: "And we desire that every one of you do shew the same diligence to the full assurance of hope unto the end." By embracing the principles of effective diligence in their respective pursuits, both hunters and Christians can achieve their goals, grow in their skills and faith, and live lives that honor God. Diligence is a journey marked by continuous effort, learning, and a commitment to thoughtful and wise decision-making, leading to success and fulfillment in both hunting and the Christian life.

Chapter 24 Duty

Duty is a fundamental concept in both hunting and the Christian life, embodying the responsibility and moral obligation to act ethically and righteously. For hunters, the duty to hunt ethically is paramount. Ethical hunting involves respecting wildlife, adhering to laws and regulations, and ensuring that one's actions do not harm the environment. This duty encompasses various aspects, such as using fair chase principles, which means giving animals a fair chance to escape, not using illegal methods or equipment, and taking clean shots to ensure a quick and humane kill. Hunters must also be mindful of conservation efforts, participating in practices that contribute to the sustainability of wildlife populations. This includes understanding and following bag limits, hunting seasons, and other regulations designed to protect species from overhunting and habitat destruction. The duty to hunt ethically extends beyond the act of hunting itself; it also involves respecting private property, being considerate of other hunters, and maintaining safety at all times. This level of responsibility requires knowledge, discipline, and a strong ethical compass, guiding hunters to make decisions that honor the natural world and the sport of hunting. Ethical hunters take pride in their duty, understanding that their actions have a significant impact on the ecosystem and the perception of hunting by the broader public.

Similarly, in the Christian life, believers are called to live righteously, fulfilling their duty to God and others. This duty is outlined in Ecclesiastes 12:13: "Let us hear the conclusion of the whole matter: Fear God, and keep his commandments: for this is the whole duty of man." This verse emphasizes the importance of revering God and adhering to His commandments as the central duty of human life. Living righteously involves following the teachings of the Bible, striving to embody the virtues of love, kindness, humility, and integrity. Christians are called to act justly, love mercy, and walk humbly with

God, as stated in Micah 6:8. This duty extends to all aspects of life, influencing how believers interact with others, make decisions, and conduct themselves in both private and public spheres. The duty to live righteously is not about rigidly following rules but about cultivating a heart and life that reflect the character of Christ. It means prioritizing spiritual growth, seeking God's will, and being a light to others through one's actions and words.

For both hunters and Christians, fulfilling their respective duties requires a combination of knowledge, commitment, and ethical principles. Hunters must be knowledgeable about the laws, regulations, and best practices of ethical hunting. This knowledge helps them to navigate the complexities of hunting responsibly, ensuring that they respect wildlife and the environment. Similarly, Christians must be knowledgeable about God's Word and the teachings of the Bible. This spiritual knowledge equips them to understand God's commandments and to live according to His will. Commitment is also essential for fulfilling one's duty. Hunters must be committed to ethical practices, even when it might be easier to take shortcuts or ignore regulations. This commitment to doing what is right reflects their respect for nature and the principles of fair chase. Similarly, Christians must be committed to living righteously, even when faced with temptations or challenges. This commitment to righteousness reflects their devotion to God and their desire to honor Him in all they do.

Both hunters and Christians benefit from the support and encouragement of their communities in fulfilling their duties. Hunters often share their experiences and knowledge with fellow hunters, learning from each other and providing mutual support. This sense of community enhances their ability to hunt ethically and responsibly. Similarly, Christians are part of a faith community that offers support, accountability, and encouragement. Fellow believers can provide wisdom, share their own experiences, and pray for one another, helping to strengthen their collective commitment to living righteously.

Hebrews 10:24-25 highlights the importance of this community support: "And let us consider one another to provoke unto love and to good works: Not forsaking the assembling of ourselves together, as the manner of some is; but exhorting one another: and so much the more, as ye see the day approaching." This sense of community helps believers to stay focused on their spiritual goals and to grow in their ability to fulfill their duty to God.

Preparation is another key aspect of fulfilling one's duty. Hunters prepare by studying their prey, practicing their skills, and planning their hunts meticulously. This preparation allows them to approach each hunt with confidence and readiness, knowing they have done everything possible to ensure ethical practices. Similarly, Christians prepare for their spiritual journey by immersing themselves in God's Word, spending time in prayer, and seeking fellowship with other believers. This spiritual preparation equips them to live righteously and to act in accordance with God's will. By being intentional about their preparation, both hunters and Christians can ensure they are well-equipped to fulfill their duties and to navigate the challenges they may face.

Reflection and learning from experiences are also crucial for fulfilling one's duty. Hunters reflect on their successes and failures, learning from each experience to improve their skills and ethical practices. This reflective practice helps them to grow in their ability to hunt responsibly and to enhance their respect for wildlife and the environment. Similarly, Christians grow in their faith by reflecting on their spiritual journey and recognizing God's faithfulness in their lives. By considering how God has guided and provided for them in the past, they can gain valuable insights and strengthen their commitment to living righteously. This reflection helps them to recognize the importance of staying committed to their spiritual journey and finding new ways to grow in their faith. Psalm 119:105 says, "Thy word is a lamp unto my feet, and a light unto my path." This verse highlights the importance of regularly engaging with Scripture to illuminate one's path and to maintain a strong commitment to fulfilling one's duty.

Both hunters and Christians must also be mindful of distractions and obstacles that can hinder their ability to fulfill their duties effectively. Hunters need to stay focused and avoid distractions that can lead them away from ethical practices or cause them to make hasty decisions. This might involve tuning out negative influences, staying focused on their objectives, and maintaining a positive mindset. Similarly, Christians must be vigilant about the influences they allow into their lives, recognizing that distractions and negative influences can lead them away from their pursuit of God's will. This vigilance involves testing the spirits, as 1 John 4:1 instructs, and being discerning about the sources of their spiritual nourishment. By maintaining a focus on God's truth and avoiding distractions, both hunters and Christians can stay committed to their goals and grow in their ability to fulfill their duties.

Adaptability is another important aspect of fulfilling one's duty. Hunters must be adaptable, ready to adjust their plans based on changing conditions, such as weather, terrain, or animal behavior. This flexibility allows them to stay focused on their goals and to respond effectively to challenges. Similarly, Christians must be adaptable in their spiritual journey, remaining open to God's leading and willing to change course when necessary. Life is full of unexpected twists and turns, and a rigid approach can lead to frustration and missed opportunities. By staying flexible and trusting in God's guidance, Christians can navigate these changes with confidence and faith.

In conclusion, duty is a fundamental aspect of success and fulfillment in both hunting and the Christian life. For hunters, fulfilling their duty to hunt ethically involves a combination of knowledge, commitment, and ethical principles, as well as the support of a knowledgeable community. For Christians, fulfilling their duty to live righteously involves regular study of Scripture, prayer, and fellowship with other believers, as well as a deep reliance on the Holy Spirit. Ecclesiastes 12:13 encapsulates this call to duty: "Let us hear the conclusion of the whole matter: Fear God, and keep his commandments: for this is the whole duty of man." By embracing the principles of fulfilling one's duty in their respective pursuits, both hunters and Christians can achieve their goals, grow in their skills and faith, and live lives that honor God. Duty is a journey marked by continuous effort, learning, and a commitment to thoughtful and wise decision-making, leading to success and fulfillment in both hunting and the Christian life.

Conclusion

As we conclude "Deer Stands and Devotions: A Hunter's Walk with God," it is my hope that this journey through the woods, both literal and spiritual, has deepened your connection with God and enriched your understanding of how the natural world can bring us closer to our Creator. The time spent in a deer stand is more than just a waiting game; it is a sacred opportunity to encounter God in the stillness, to listen to His voice, and to reflect on the many ways He reveals Himself through His creation.

Throughout this book, we have explored the spiritual lessons that emerge from the hunting experience—lessons of patience, discipline, humility, and reverence. These virtues are not only essential to a successful hunt but are also key components of a thriving spiritual life. As hunters, we know the importance of being prepared, of understanding the environment, and of respecting the creatures we pursue. Similarly, in our walk with God, we must be spiritually prepared, attuned to the environment of our hearts, and respectful of the life and purpose He has given us.

The deer stand, often seen as a place of solitude, becomes a place of communion with God when we bring our hearts and minds into His presence. In the quiet moments before dawn, as the world awakens around us, we are reminded of God's faithfulness in creation and His constant presence in our lives. The same God who set the stars in place, who designed the intricate patterns of a deer's coat, is the God who walks with us through every season, every challenge, and every triumph.

As you step out of the woods and back into the busyness of daily life, I encourage you to carry the lessons learned in the deer stand with you. Let the patience you've cultivated guide you as you wait on God's timing in your life. Let the discipline required for a successful hunt remind you of the importance of spiritual disciplines like prayer and

Scripture study. And let the reverence you feel in the presence of God's creation inspire a deeper worship and appreciation for the Creator Himself.

Whether you're in a deer stand, walking through the woods, or sitting in your living room, remember that God is with you, ready to speak to your heart, ready to reveal Himself in new and profound ways.

As you continue your journey, may you find that the quiet moments spent in nature have prepared you to hear God's voice more clearly, to trust His guidance more fully, and to walk with Him more closely. Just as you have learned to read the signs in the woods, may you also learn to recognize the signs of God's presence in your everyday life. And may your walk with God be as rich and rewarding as any hunt, filled with moments of awe, gratitude, and deep, abiding peace.

Don't miss out!

Visit the website below and you can sign up to receive emails whenever Joshua Rhoades publishes a new book. There's no charge and no obligation.

https://books2read.com/r/B-A-AJLBB-PUBYE

BOOKS 2 READ

Connecting independent readers to independent writers.

Did you love *Deer Stands and Devotions: A Hunter's Walk with God*? Then you should read *HOOK, LINE & SAVIOUR - Faith Reflections from Fishing*[1] by Joshua Rhoades!

"Hook, Line, and Saviour: Faith Reflections from Fishing" is an engaging book for both the young and not so young, blending fishing with Christian faith principles. Through 24 chapters, it draws parallels between fishing techniques and the Christian life, making spiritual lessons relatable and fun.It starts with "Chapter 1 - Research and Knowledge," emphasizing the importance of understanding and preparation in both fishing and faith. "Chapter 2 - Choosing the Right Gear" draws a parallel between selecting the right fishing tools and using spiritual tools like prayer and scripture."Chapter 3 - Learning to Cast" highlights the need for skill and practice, comparing it to sharing

1. https://books2read.com/u/brjDGE

2. https://books2read.com/u/brjDGE

one's faith. "Chapter 4 - Understanding Weather Conditions" connects the importance of weather awareness for fishing to understanding spiritual and emotional climates. "Chapter 5 - Tide and Water Currents" uses tides to illustrate how life's changes can be navigated with trust in God.In "Chapter 6 - Selecting the Right Bait," using the right bait attracts fish, just as kindness and love draw others to faith. "Chapter 7 - Tackle Box Organization" underscores being spiritually organized and prepared. "Chapter 8 - Knot Tying" emphasizes building strong relationships with God and others, like tying secure knots."Chapter 9 - Boat Maintenance" compares maintaining faith through prayer to keeping a boat in good condition. "Chapter 10 - Fishing Regulations" highlights adhering to God's commandments, like following fishing laws. "Chapter 11 - Fish Finder Technology" parallels using technology to locate fish with seeking guidance through prayer."Chapter 12 - Patience and Persistence" teaches that both fishing and faith require waiting and perseverance. "Chapter 13 - Observation Skills" encourages attentiveness to God's work, like a fisherman watches for fish. "Chapter 14 - Casting Techniques" and "Chapter 15 - Reeling Techniques" relate fishing skills to guiding others to faith."Chapter 16 - Fishing Ethics" emphasizes integrity and honesty in fishing and life. "Chapter 17 - Adapting to Seasons" discusses embracing God's plan through life's phases. "Chapter 18 - Using Scents and Attractants" highlights living a life that draws others to Christ."Chapter 19 - Fishing Logs" suggests keeping a faith journal to track growth. "Chapter 20 - Joining a Fishing Community" underscores fellowship and support. "Chapter 21 - Safety Precautions" parallels physical safety measures in fishing with spiritual protection."Chapter 22 - Learning from Experts" encourages seeking wisdom from mentors. "Chapter 23 - Adapting to Different Waters" relates to being adaptable in life. "Chapter 24 - Staying Informed" emphasizes continuous spiritual growth.Overall, "Hook, Line, and Saviour" makes learning about faith accessible and enjoyable. Through practical application it encourages spiritual growth and helps readers apply Christian principles in daily life. This book is an adventurous guide that deepens faith through the exciting world of fishing, making spiritual growth enriching and fun.